CORPORATE GOVERNANCE AND THE BOARD — WHAT WORKS BEST

Prepared by

PRICEWATERHOUSECOOPERS

Principal Authors
Richard M. Steinberg, *Project Leader*
Catherine L. Bromilow, *Project Manager*

Project Sponsor
John W. Copley

Sponsored by
The Institute of Internal Auditors Research Foundation

Disclosure

The IIA RF publishes this document for informational and educational purposes. This document is intended to provide information, but is not a substitute for legal or accounting advice. The IIA does not provide such advice and makes no warranty as to any legal or accounting results through its publication of this document. When legal or accounting issues arise, professional assistance should be sought and retained.

ISBN 0-89413-438-8
00191 05/00
First Printing

CONTENTS

About the Authors v
About the Team vii
About This Report ix
How to Use It xi

Chapter 1 — Strategy and Planning 1

Chapter 2 — Risk Management 11

Chapter 3 — Tone at the Top 19

Chapter 4 — Measuring and Monitoring Performance 27

Chapter 5 — Transformational Transactions 37

Chapter 6 — Management Evaluation, Compensation, and Succession Planning 47

Chapter 7 — Telling the World 57

Chapter 8 — Board Dynamics 65

Appendix A — Self-Assessment Guide 77
Appendix B — Project Method 95
Appendix C — Selected Bibliography 101

IIA Research Foundation Board of Trustees 1999/2000 105
IIA Research Foundation Board of Research Advisors 1999/2000 107

ABOUT THE AUTHORS

Richard M. Steinberg

Rick Steinberg is a senior partner of PricewaterhouseCoopers LLP and its Professional, Technical, Risk & Quality Leader for Corporate Governance, responsible for design and development of PwC's corporate governance program, thought leadership, and serving major companies on governance and related issues.

Mr. Steinberg is a founder of his firm's risk management and control consulting practice and served as its global leader, overseeing development of client service capabilities around the world and serving as senior resource on international engagements. In addition to leading this study, *Corporate Governance and the Board – What Works Best*, he served as lead project partner on the team that developed the landmark study, *Internal Control – Integrated Framework*, published by the Committee of Sponsoring Organizations of the Treadway Commission (COSO) and which has gained recognition as *the* standard of internal control. He led the development of GLOBE, PwC's interactive system providing leading-edge industry, best practice and benchmarking information to PwC's client service professionals worldwide.

Mr. Steinberg has long been a leader in shaping professional standards, serving as chair, co-chair or member of many committees and task forces of the American Institute of CPAs. He is a member of the Conference Board's Global Corporate Governance Research Center Advisory Board, and was selected by COSO to serve on its Advisory Council for developing guidance on specialized business issues. He is widely published, authoring books, monographs and articles in leading journals, and is a sought-after speaker by business, professional and academic organizations. He is a graduate of the University of Pennsylvania's Wharton School, holds an MBA from New York University's Graduate School of Business, and is recognized in *Who's Who in Finance and Industry.*

Catherine L. Bromilow

Catherine Bromilow is a senior manager with the Corporate Governance Services group of PricewaterhouseCoopers LLP. She works with boards of directors of major companies and institutions bringing best practice and enhancing programs to comply with evolving regulations and expectations. Most recently she has worked with audit committees, benchmarking processes and performance against the Blue Ribbon Committee recommendations and best practice.

Ms. Bromilow was the project manager for this study, *Corporate Governance and The Board — What Works Best.* She has had management responsibility on audit and consulting engagements in the U.S. and Canada, and was selected for secondment to the Canada Deposit Insurance Corporation. Previously, she served as internal audit manager at the Toronto-Dominion Bank, assisting the bank to achieve its risk management, corporate governance and regulatory compliance objectives.

Ms. Bromilow speaks at international conferences and seminars on corporate governance, compliance, ethics and risk management, and has lectured at the university level. She is a Chartered Accountant from Canada and holds both Master of Accounting and BA (Honours Chartered Accountancy Studies) degrees from the University of Waterloo.

ABOUT THE TEAM

This book is sponsored and published as a part of The IIA Research Foundation's Master Key series. The IIA (www.theiia.org) is the internal auditing profession's acknowledged leader, recognized authority, and chief educator. The Foundation mirrors The IIA's leadership by providing internal auditing practitioners, executive management, and corporate governance entities with valuable materials such as this book and its counterpart, *Audit Committee Effectiveness — What Works Best, 2nd Edition.*

PricewaterhouseCoopers is proud of our collaboration with The IIA Research Foundation and our authorship of this study, *Corporate Governance and the Board — What Works Best.* PricewaterhouseCoopers (www.pwcglobal.com) is the world's largest professional services organization. Drawing on the knowledge and skills of more than 150,000 people in 150 countries, we help our clients solve complex business problems and measurably enhance their ability to build value, manage risk, and improve performance in an Internet-enabled world. PricewaterhouseCoopers refers to the member firms of the worldwide PricewaterhouseCoopers organization.

Advisory Team
Charles H. Allen
LeRoy E. Bookal, CIA
Michael Cangemi
Stephen A. Doherty
Gareth Evans
Jane F. Mutchler
Claire Beth Nilsen
Tage Rasmussen

The Institute of Internal Auditors
Headquarters Staff
William G. Bishop III, CIA,
President, The Institute of Internal Auditors
Basil H. Pflumm, CIA, *Vice President, Practices Center;*
Executive Director, The IIA Research Foundation
Eugene J. O'Neill, CIA, *Director of Finance and Customer Services*
Susan B. Lione, CIA, *Senior Manager, Research*
Roland Laing, *Manager, Technical Services*
Trish W. Harris, *Senior Manager, Corporate Marketing,*
Media Relations and Public Relations
Wendy Acha, *Research Administrator*

ABOUT THIS REPORT

Board effectiveness, long debated, has become a red-hot topic. Boards of companies suffering a crisis or lackluster performance especially have felt the heat. There has been no shortage of recommendations for improvement, with directors inundated with materials, seminars and roundtables. But advice has focused largely on board structure, addressing composition, size, member independence, committees and other issues that, although important, don't get at the heart of the matter. Volumes also have been written on the broader concept of corporate governance, defined as encompassing all stakeholders including regulators, management, employees, auditors and society at large.

In contrast, this report is about the *board*—and advises directors on *what* the board needs to do and *how* best to do it. It describes responsibilities boards must embrace and provides leading-edge direction on how best to meet those responsibilities. The focus is on shareholder value. Although this guidance will help satisfy other stakeholders, it doesn't deal directly with them. It homes in on how to be most *effective in enhancing shareholder value.*

The report has been developed with face-to-face input from some of the most experienced, savvy directors anywhere on the globe. With that, along with ideas of corporate governance thought leaders, survey of board members and PricewaterhouseCoopers' own experience with leading companies and their boards, we've put together the best of the best. It might be called "best practice," but indeed no board, even those of successful companies with the largest capitalizations, is utilizing everything suggested here.

For those reasons, even knowledgeable, experienced directors of major companies will find in this report new ways of getting the job done better. Yes, they'll see practices their boards have used successfully, but we venture to say every director will take away important new information—some that may well make a difference in their board's and company's success. Ideas not embraced can at least trigger discussion and debate, resulting in increased board effectiveness.

To be clear, this report does not set a common standard, and certainly not a minimum one. It draws from board practices of companies around the world, but does not recognize differences in country culture or board structure. It sets the bar at the *highest* level to make a board *most effective* in enhancing shareholder value—commensurate with the best of today's boards' resources and shareholder expectations. Accordingly, some boards will find they need to jump much higher to measure up, whereas the best boards can reach the goal of broad-based excellence more easily and quickly.

Will adopting these practices reduce director liability? The best answer is "yes," but not because of any particular attention paid to law and regulation. Rather, because boards will indeed become more effective, which by itself reduces legal exposure. Conversely, this report in no way sets any legal standard.

What to do? We guess you will begin by scanning a few pages, but—at the risk of sounding presumptuous—we believe you'll find yourself spending more time with this report than anticipated. We trust you will find leading-edge practices, even a few gems, you'll want to act on immediately.

PricewaterhouseCoopers LLP

HOW TO USE IT

With directors among the most time-pressured executives, this report is designed to minimize reading effort. It's written in a crisp, easy style, and organized to let you go directly to areas of greatest interest.

So, we suggest you jump right into whichever chapters are most compelling. There are no prerequisites.

What's in the Chapter

Strategy and Planning

Once-proud companies and boards have learned that bad strategy can kill. You'll read about impediments to effective strategy development, and what does and doesn't work. The chapter differentiates "incremental," "substantial" and "transformational" strategies and points to critical information needs. It shares insights on why and how the best boards not only shape strategy, but also scrutinize the development *process* and plans for *implementation*.

Risk Management

Boards must know where risk exists, and what management's doing about it. The chapter shows how innovative companies view risk not solely as hazards, but also as controlling uncertainty and *seizing opportunity*. It highlights board oversight in developing an effective risk management *architecture*, including pitfalls and what needs to go right. And it outlines why the board needs to make sure responsibility and accountability are in exactly the right place.

Tone at the Top

Unethical behavior ultimately damages companies and their people. By contrast, operating with integrity and high ethical values is good business—those companies draw the best people and most sought-after customer and supplier relationships, and find open doors to critical alliances, partnerships and merger candidates. The chapter shows directors how to find out what's *really* going on, and steps management must take. Also covered are the ethics of merger candidates—and why that's doubly important—ethics in time of change, and how directors *themselves* must behave.

Measuring and Monitoring Performance

Leading boards look less at after-the-fact yardsticks, more at nonfinancial leading indicators that drive value. You'll see how to make sure your company's measures are aligned with tactical and strategic plans, all linked to value drivers and rewards. Also highlighted are principles underlying effective performance measurement, key information requirements, and how to get past the daunting challenges of getting the measurement process right.

Transformational Transactions

Most acquisitions represent huge bets that don't pay off—they actually reduce share value. What to do, with access to target information severely limited and negotiation timeframes so tight they challenge the bounds of common sense? The chapter shows how some boards get it right, avoiding typical fault lines of flawed strategy, due diligence and post-deal implementation. It identifies pitfalls, and where boards must direct attention. And you'll read about divestitures and alliances, looking at the partner, deal structure and needed homework.

Management Evaluation, Compensation and Succession Planning

Even experienced directors feel uneasy evaluating the CEO. But nothing is more important than getting this right. The chapter outlines a constructive process linking the CEO's personal development plan with performance targets and strategy, requiring a long-term vision for the company while still keeping an eye on short-term performance and rewards. It outlines how savvy directors assess the intangibles and get the compensation package right in an environment of economic and market volatility. And it describes how boards come to grips with a need to replace a forceful and powerful chief executive, and handle succession planning.

Telling the World: External Communications

Increased global competition for capital cries for greater disclosure and "transparency," and sharpens regulators' focus on earnings manipulation and board oversight. Analysts are demanding more nonfinancial, operating data—information not subject to companies' normal reliability review processes. You'll read how boards help their companies avoid communications problems, including challenges posed by technology. The chapter summarizes key elements boards monitor in the communications process, and how they can protect the company against loose lips when major transactions are brewing.

Board Dynamics

The days of rubber stamping management's decisions, collecting fees and adjourning for lunch are over. Unlike failures, which attract attention, good boards function quietly and efficiently in growing long-term shareholder value. But boards can't succeed if they're dysfunctional—and few are perfect. This chapter speaks to the good and the bad, identifying make or break characteristics in CEO/board relations. It also shows how boards and individual directors self-assess performance—and how the process can truly work well—and concludes with board renewal and director commitment.

Do Committees Count?

Yes. Most boards use committees—audit, nominating, governance, executive, compensation—to deal with specified responsibilities. It allows greater attention than the full board can give, and targets experience and expertise. But because committee structure uniquely fits the needs and composition of each board, this report gives particular committees only passing reference. The full board is ultimately accountable for all board responsibilities, and we look here at how boards—in whatever subsets are deemed best—operate most effectively.

How Much Involvement?

In reading this report it's useful to keep in mind a theme running throughout—the degree of board involvement with management. At one extreme, some boards are "hands off"—they periodically review performance, and if results are satisfactory they keep on monitoring. If not, they change management. At the other extreme, some directors are involved with management virtually day-to-day.

Which is best? Neither extreme typically is successful. With the velocity of change in today's environment, the first approach—acting after the fact—finds the damage long since done. The second is meddling to the extent of not letting management do its job.

Some suggest the best place is the middle of the spectrum. But we believe not. Boards need to operate at right of center, for two reasons. First—again because of the rapidly changing environment—boards must be proactive to add necessary value. They must lean toward more timely involvement than less. And second, the right board members bring critically needed expertise, experience and judgment to bear on issues determining the company's success or failure. Managements need all the help they can get, and there's often no better place than the board to find the skills and company-based knowledge to make a positive difference.

How Is Our Board Doing?

A self-assessment guide allows you quickly to see how well your board stacks up against these leading practices.

CHAPTER 1
STRATEGY AND PLANNING

While CEOs recognize that developing "the right" strategy is extremely difficult, and consistently rank strategy as one of their top issues, a poll of directors shows board contribution to strategic planning is lacking. Indeed, it is the area most needing improvement. Effective boards play a critical role in the development process, by both ensuring a sound strategic planning process and scrutinizing the plan itself with the rigor required to determine whether it deserves endorsement.

A wide range of views exists among directors on what's the right extent of board involvement in strategy development. One director describes his view: "If the board isn't comfortable with the strategy that management has set, it should tell management to rethink it, and come back with something better. But, the board shouldn't be involved in developing the strategy. That is, noses in, fingers out."

But prevailing thinking among experienced directors drives behavior in a different direction. They are actively involved with management in setting corporate strategy.

Impediments to Effective Strategy Development

Headlines are filled with stories of well-known, respected companies that imploded due to strategic failures. How could well-intentioned, seasoned executives create strategies that became, ultimately, competitive disadvantages? And how could directors have approved them?

Looking at past practice, a large part of the answer can be found in dysfunctional management/board dynamics. Board members point to CEO/chairs who:

- Set a highly controlled agenda for strategy discussions, creating an environment making it difficult for independent directors to raise concerns about critical strategic issues.
- Became intractably committed to one strategy to the exclusion of other possibilities, and were impatient with directors not sharing total commitment to the chosen path.
- Were reluctant to acknowledge past mistakes, hanging onto a poor strategy, with resulting stagnation at the company.

On the other hand, directors have contributed to a failed process, being hesitant to aggressively and constructively challenge management-developed strategy. In many cases this was because directors were not sufficiently prepared, or felt they might be violating established norms of boardroom debate, fearing they would find themselves isolated and perhaps ultimately replaced. Some directors' reluctance was due at least in part to the reality that management had better, more in-depth understanding of the industry and company, with significant time and resources not immediately available to the board. It has been noted, interestingly, that this very proximity to the business can prevent management from seeing critical factors and seriously considering important alternatives.

What Works

Despite inherent difficulties presented by board/management dynamics, many boards do a great job in ensuring a successful strategy. What do effective boards do?

They strike a balance based on a clear distinction between the role of the board and that of management, where the board provides oversight and strategic insights, while avoiding "micro-managing" or dramatically slowing the strategic decision-making process. Among the key roles that a board plays in the strategy development process are:

- Reviewing options, challenging them, adding additional perspective and agreeing on appropriate measures for success.
- Reviewing the strategy development process to ensure it is sufficiently robust to consider the appropriate range of alternatives and to assess them properly.
- Examining plans and processes for strategy implementation.
- Monitoring implementation through agreed metrics and providing operational and tactical guidance to management.

Done well, these can improve strategy and in fact *speed* the decision-making process, by ensuring consensus on the strategy and driving investment and operating decisions supportive of that direction.

Effective boards also practice the fundamentals. They have an effective working partnership with management in developing and reviewing the corporate strategy. These boards bring insight, knowledge, judgment and analytical skill to the strategic planning process, focusing on critical issues such as emerging customer preferences, technology risks and opportunities, quality issues, supply chain enhancement needs, electronic commerce and other emerging market channels, and new product and market opportunities.

These directors constructively challenge alternatives put forth, in a way management willingly embraces, because the right working relationship has already been established. One director summarized the board's role: "Board members must be strong enough to stand up to management yet be friendly and cooperative. Their role should be one of cooperative and spirited oversight. They cannot be rubber stamps."

Boards use any of a number of vehicles to fulfill their responsibility for reviewing, understanding and approving company strategy.

Board Meeting Discussions. The most common venue for board discussion of strategy is still the regular board meeting. But an important drawback is that regular meeting agendas cover too many other topics, and don't allow sufficient time for full understanding and discussion of the strategic plan. One director notes, "Agendas can be a challenge because they don't allow for sufficient focus on the important strategic issues facing the company." Another points out that the board on which he serves "spends too much time on results and not enough focusing on strategy." Even though this company is successful, he feels a greater focus on the future is needed.

Special Board-Level Strategy Meetings. A number of leading companies hold special board-level strategy meetings. These meetings provide enough time, two days being common, during which the strategy is thoroughly explored and discussed. These sessions typically are conducted off site, providing an environment conducive to success.

Empowering a Board Committee. Some boards delegate responsibility for strategy to a board committee (such as a strategy or finance committee, or an executive committee). The committee's findings are presented to and discussed with the full board, which, when satisfied, provides its approval. Other boards insist all directors be involved, because of the extreme importance of strategy to company success.

Advisory Groups. Some leading organizations form advisory groups or councils to advise both senior management and the board. These sometimes have widespread representation, providing cultural, political and economic perspectives. More importantly, they include individuals with expertise in areas critical to where the business wants to go. These advisory groups have proven especially valuable in counseling on multinational strategy issues, particularly related to global markets. In addition to providing the organization access to global thought leaders, this approach avoids pressure to increase board size by adding additional specialized expertise.

Facilitation. Strategy design often is supported by outside specialists with expertise in strategic development, the industry and facilitation.

These approaches are not mutually exclusive. Many directors favor an off-site meeting with knowledgeable, experienced facilitators, attended by senior management and either the entire board or a large enough segment to bring the necessary perspective, challenge and judgment to bear.

The Board Needs Relevant Information and Analysis

To effectively review and evaluate strategy, directors must consider a great deal of information beyond the draft strategic plan itself. Effective boards critically review the content and sufficiency of supporting information. A governance thought leader comments, "Directors need complete information—on products, customers' views, market conditions, as well as on critical strategic and organizational issues. We need to be particularly wary of strategies that are positioned as surefire, can't fail or risk free."

Although management typically strives to provide the board with all relevant information, experienced directors consider what's not there, and proactively seek out what may be missing—anything that will help them properly evaluate strategy. And they insist on receiving information timely. One director said, "If directors are not getting good information in advance and of the nature they want, it's a warning signal. Directors need to insist that they get what they ask for." Exhibit 1.1 identifies information successful boards typically look for in assessing the strategy.

Exhibit 1.1: Information Boards Need to Fulfill Strategy-Related Responsibilities

Internally Produced

- **Alternate Strategies:** options considered by management and with comparative analysis
- **Strategic Plan:** clear statement of proposed strategy and how management plans to implement
- **Performance Measures:** targets for key non-financial and financial measures. In subsequent years, the board will use these measures to evaluate the strategy's success.
- **Major Risk Factors:** internal and external factors that could prevent the company from achieving the strategy, including likelihood and magnitude of the risks and means by which management will address them.
- **Major Interdependencies:** related strategic initiatives with suppliers, customers or partners, along with associated risk information.
- **Resources and Investments Required:** including people, capital and capacity and tied to the sources of funding for any major new investments called for in the strategy.
- **Divestiture of Existing Businesses Required:** should be identified and addressed.
- **Strategic Alliances, Partnerships and Acquisitions:** those needed for successful implementation must be identified, with implementation plans
- **Technology Implications:** dependence on, need for and opportunities related to expanded use of technology, with its high level of associated risk. Electronic commerce issues should be clearly highlighted.
- **Best, Worst and Most Likely Case Scenarios:** related to the assessment of risks inherent in the strategy. Could also indicate the degree of stretch beyond current performance required to achieve the strategy.
- **Evaluation of Past Strategies:** including identification of successful strategies and an analysis of elements that were not successful.

From External Sources

- **Current and Evolving Customer Demand:** with focus on the future.
- **Company's Current Market Position:** i.e., its major products and services, as well as its sources of competitive advantage.
- **Competitor Intelligence:** major current and expected future competitors and a comparison of relative strengths, competitive advantages and strategies.
- **Industry Information and Trends:** including the expected impact of technology and electronic commerce.
- **Analysis of Potential Stakeholder Reaction:** including shareholders, to the proposed strategy, considering major stakeholder response to similar past moves.
- **Information on Concerns:** expressed by market analysts and the media.

The last two items should include management's plans to address significant concerns that might arise from these sources.

What the Board Should Look for

While successful strategies vary widely, commonalities exist. Among the critical issues sophisticated directors look at include whether the strategy developers have effectively dealt with:

- Major forces shaping the competitive landscape, including globalization, electronic business, disruptive technologies and innovation, and convergence of industries.
- The changing rules of the competitive game, where competitive advantage is short-lived.
- Worldwide deregulation and decontrol of product and financial markets.

To what extent is change sought? Change can be *incremental, substantial or transformational.* Using a basketball analogy, incremental change involves better ball handling and shooting. Substantial change involves calling new plays, perhaps with new players. Transformational change redefines the game.

In business terms:

Incremental change often occurs through *operational alignment*, accompanied by "right sizing" and cost reduction, aligning processes with a market and product focus.

Substantial change may involve *repositioning*, or a new market/product focus, factoring in competitive trends, best practices in the same or other industries, and company strengths/shortcomings. This is what most people mean when they talk in terms of "strategy." Substantial change may drive a company to a *high performance organization*, where successfully redefining and realigning processes with market and product repositioning create significant value.

Transformational change is achieved by "breakthrough" strategy, which combines the above and goes beyond by changing the competitive conditions of the industry. The company builds a core competence that transcends current industry practice, creating new market/product opportunities, often implying an entirely new business.

Examples of successful breakthrough strategy include Toyota's lean production system, Intel's high-velocity product development and Amazon.com's Internet-based distribution channels. Done well, a breakthrough strategy can generate tremendous shareholder value.

Using this context, directors can assess what form of change is desired or necessitated by economic, social, market and competitor forces, and seek strategy development that's right for their company. Knowledge of what makes a successful strategy work is critical. For example, experience shows that breakthrough strategy is difficult to achieve organically, and while acquisitions can be useful, they too often fail to meet expectations.

The tack to take will be based on the corporate vision, accompanied by a thorough analysis of competitive positioning, including:

- Where to compete, looking at markets (customer segmentation and targeting), products (portfolio life cycle management and margin targets), and channels (value-added channels and e-commerce).
- How to compete, looking at the industry value chain (supplier strategy, company domain, channel strategy) and financial structure, including cash flow strategy.

Also important are internal capabilities, including corporate culture, core processes, people, capital, technology, systems and organizational structure.

Successful boards look for these analyses, and how they are used in strategy development. Used effectively, the resulting strategy is conceptually sound, market focused and grounded in what the company is today and needs to be for success going forward.

Don't Ignore the Process

Effective boards ensure they are comfortable not only with the information and analyses used by management in strategy development, but also with the strategic planning *process*. Directors consider major activities, planning timeframe, steps involved and the extent to which key members of management participated in strategy development. These reviews identify outside participants, such as consultants, as well as means used, such as scenario analysis or focus groups, and how that information was used.

Directors need to be confident the strategy to be adopted will result in superior shareholder value creation. It should be designed to generate greater shareholder value than other strategy alternatives. It should ensure long-term viability of the company, or identify a potentially critical need for business combination. The strategic plan also should clearly define how shareholder value creation will be measured.

Effective strategic planning considers associated risks and management's plan for managing those risks. Risk is a double-edged sword. In today's world taking too little risk can be as dangerous as taking too much. The company must take enough risk to seize opportunities and remain competitive in the face of quickly changing markets, product innovation, delivery channels, methods of doing business and nimble competitors.

In the end, the board must be comfortable with the process used to develop the strategy, with the strategy itself, and that management—beyond just the CEO— buys into it and is committed to its successful implementation. While successful boards become "thought partners" with management in strategy development, it is management that must own the strategic plan and fully believe in it.

Watch the Linkage

Shareholder value creation will occur when the right strategy is directly linked to value drivers, the tactical plan and risk management of critical business processes. This linkage is pictured in Exhibit 1.2, with each element addressed in succeeding chapters.

Exhibit 1.2: Linking Strategy to Shareholder Value

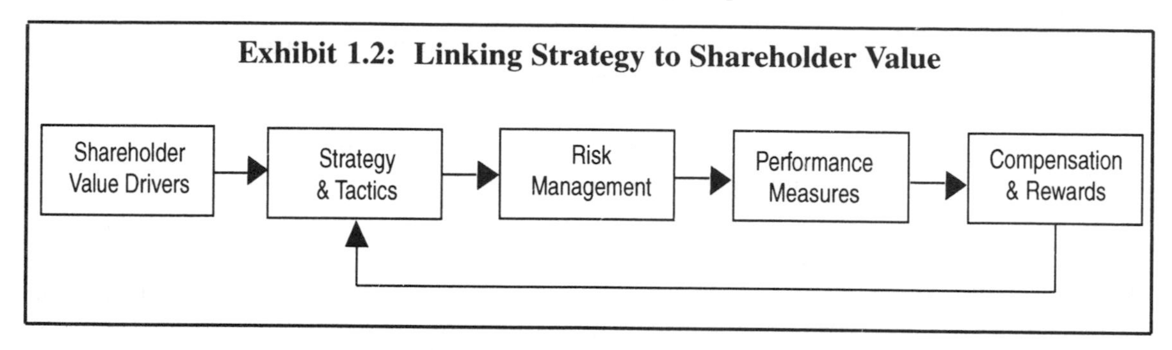

Nothing Is More Important Than Successful Implementation

"The best laid plans . . . " As important as having a great strategy is, plans for effective implementation are as important, and can be more elusive. This is where boards often fail to focus sufficient attention, and serious problems germinate and fester.

Implementation plans must necessarily drive change through the company. What do effective boards look for in implementation planning? They look for well-constructed plans for:

- Realigning the organization to make it happen. Business units, support infrastructures and processes typically need to be realigned, and sometimes revamped or disbanded.
- Effective use of technology, in marketing and selling, supply chain logistics, design and manufacturing, and customer and support services. Electronic commerce is a major focus of most successful strategies today, and timely and effective implementation can make the difference.
- Recruiting, developing and retaining the human talent and skills necessary to drive toward where the new strategy demands, and putting the right people in key roles managing the business. Incentive, compensation and assessment processes must be in place to make this work effectively.
- Managing the knowledge necessary for quick and effective customer care, risk management and innovation, so that the right information is in the hands of the right people at the right time. The notion that we live in a knowledge economy has never been more true.
- Global implementation, with in-depth and current knowledge of emerging customer demands and local business practice know-how, and the resources, organization and facilities to succeed.

- Effective risk management, with the right mechanisms in place to identify barriers and opportunities that assuredly will arise sooner than anticipated.

Successful boards spend considerable time understanding and constructively challenging the implementation, or the "business" or "operating" plan. Rather than a cursory or ad hoc approach, these boards apply a disciplined approach to reviewing and becoming comfortable with the plan. They know whether "slack" is built into plans—allowing operating management to meet goals with little effort—and push for more aggressive targets if needed to achieve shareholder value goals.

Similar to the strategy review process, directors must have access to a wide range of information to effectively assess an operating plan. This typically includes well-defined action plans, with responsibilities and timeframes, to address critical drivers such as those outlined above. In addition, routine management information, although more mundane, must be reviewed to ensure consistency and alignment. That information is outlined in Exhibit 1.3.

Exhibit 1.3: Information Boards Need to Fulfill Operating Plan-Related Responsibilities

• Financial Budgets:	Should include all operating and capital budgets and details on funding sources for major programs or company initiatives. Budgetary information should include targets and details for key financial statement amounts, as well as targets for financial ratios important for industry or financial markets. Details supporting the consolidated plan, such as budgets by division or business, should be included.
• Key Driver Performance Measures:	Individual performance measures should be clearly explained, and related targets explicitly set. The board should understand whether an individual target is a "floor" or a "ceiling," or an exact target.
• Key Risks:	Should include identification and assessment of the probability of risks occurring, their potential impact and how management intends to manage them.
• Major Assumptions:	Used in preparing the plan, with an analysis of likelihood and impact of potential deviations.

As with strategy development, implementation plans must have the full buy-in and commitment of the people who will be carrying them out. Key players at all organizational levels should come together, preferably in cross-functional teams, to specify what they must do day-to-day for successful implementation. They are then positioned to use operating measures and targets to manage against the new strategy.

CHAPTER 2
RISK MANAGEMENT

With the possible exception of strategy development, the topic most discussed at the board level today is *risk.* Boards want to know where risk exists, and what's being done about it.

Directors have seen how some of the world's best-known companies have endured great pain associated with unanticipated risk—ranging from product failures to blunders with legal or regulatory compliance to technology or physical disasters. They want to sleep comfortably knowing major surprises won't hit their company.

What most comes to mind when considering the term *risk* is the possibility of something bad happening. Risk has long been associated with catastrophic insurable events, as well as financial institutions' exposure to market, credit, liquidity and other negative occurrences. In recent years, companies have focused on specific areas of potential loss, such as executing sophisticated financial transactions, including "derivatives," and legal and regulatory compliance.

The perception of risk has now evolved to cover a much wider scope—emerging technology, political, economic, competitive or industry issues, as well as internally sourced risks. And the concept of risk no longer is limited to bad things that might occur. Sophisticated managements are taking a holistic view of risk and risk management, better positioning their companies for success.

The Evolutionary Risk Continuum

Where is your company on the risk continuum that runs from *hazard* through *uncertainty* to *opportunity*? Most companies focus on preventing major *hazards* that can blow a hole in operating results or generate huge liabilities. Many are proactive in identifying what might go wrong, managing the risk through insurance coverage or mitigating it with specific actions and internal controls.

An increasing number of companies look at a wide range of *uncertainties*, shoring up operational processes and instituting programs, as well as controls, to deal with potential negatives that can stand in the way of achieving desired results.

But fewer managements have broadened their perspective to see the flip slide of risk as *opportunity*. Simply put, every business enterprise must take some risk in order to reap desired rewards. The better a company is at identifying and managing risk, the more ready and able it is to take prudent risks. Managements of those companies seize the right opportunities, because they are justifiably comfortable taking bold steps essential to success in today's environment. More on this later.

The Board's Role

The board is not directly responsible for risk management. Management has that responsibility. But the board needs to be certain that that responsibility is carried out—effectively, proactively and ongoing. Reality, however, is that few companies have a disciplined process for doing this. Usually done ad hoc, many risks are identified, often on a timely basis. But an ad hoc approach is not good enough, because too often serious risks are not seen until it's too late, and the result can be devastating. Boards believing their companies were making simple hedges to guard against major currency or other rate fluctuations weren't aware until too late that huge, uncovered bets were on the table. Boards didn't know about improper sales practices, or new products from emerging competitors about to seize market share, or new highly profitable channel or market opportunities unnecessarily missed.

What, then, are the board's major responsibilities?

- First, to see that the organization has in place an effective, ongoing *process* to identify risk, measure its potential impact against a varied set of assumptions and do what's necessary to proactively manage it.
- Second, the board also must be certain it is apprised of the most significant risks, and determine for each whether the right actions are being taken.

Reality is that boards focus much more on the second responsibility than the first. Directors typically ask management about critical risks, and discussion ensues about actions planned or taken. But directors cannot be sure all key risks are discussed if they don't have confidence in the company's ability to surface them. Only a handful of boards are looking at management's process to proactively find and deal with significant risks.

A director of one company laments, "Our board isn't dealing with risk in a systematic, broad manner and isn't addressing the entire universe of risks associated with strategy, culture, people." Another director makes a similar point: "Management has a tendency to report on risks selectively and directors must be wary of management omissions. We have to understand the issues that impact the company's long term success."

What to Look for in the Process

A number of companies have established effective risk management processes, and while they are different, there are commonalties. Their successful implementation provides a good roadmap for board focus.

These companies have followed a conceptually straightforward approach of aligning their strategy, business objectives, risks, actions and controls.

- Starting with the corporate strategic plan, management identifies, by strategic initiative or business segment, the major objectives that if achieved will successfully implement the strategy and achieve the targeted operational and financial results.
- Management then looks at the risks related to those objectives. That is, it identifies the barriers, or things that could go wrong, and critical success factors that must go right to provide the greatest likelihood of success.
- Next management decides what initiatives, programs or other actions are needed to deal with the risks in a positive, proactive way.
- Controls are identified or designed to ensure the actions are in fact carried out as planned.
- The entire process is monitored over time, promoting its successful achievement.

While simple in concept, implementation of a robust risk management process is another story. Particular attention is needed to reaching consensus among managers even on what should be self-evident, such as what the objectives of a business unit are and which managers "own" which processes. Several methodologies are used to achieve the desired alignment, many entailing facilitated sessions to bring key people together, enabling the requisite "buy-in" to make it work.

The end game is the establishment of a "risk architecture" or "risk framework" throughout each of the business units and levels of the company. That is, the board will want to be sure management has not only identified existing risks and is managing them—akin to a "snapshot" at a point in time—but also established a process that is effective at identifying new risks as they emerge. This framework doesn't have to be a separate process superimposed on top of existing management processes, and indeed should not be. Rather, it should be integrated within the way management runs the business, enriching that process and making it risk-focused. When done well, an enterprise-wide risk management architecture ensures risks are properly managed, assets secured, reputation protected, and shareholder value enhanced.

Pitfalls

A board overseeing management's development of a risk management architecture should be aware of pitfalls that can derail implementation.

- Not using common terminology, so participants talk and act at cross-purposes. Virtually everyone has a different internal definition of risk, and terms like *operational, compliance* and *financial reporting* risk need to be understood by all.
- Shortcutting the process, focusing first on risk. A common trap, this results in addressing many issues having little to do with the company's real strategic objectives.
- Putting implementation responsibility at too low an organizational level. To be truly effective, senior management must be actively supportive.
- Failing to eliminate programs not aligned with the identified objectives. Companies continue to engage in activities and initiatives geared to long-outdated goals. Effective application of this methodology will identify and eliminate unnecessary work.
- Taking the "snapshot" approach without following through to embed an ongoing risk management architecture into the organization. Linking objectives with current risks is a good start, but it's necessary to establish mechanisms to identify risks that will arise in the future and could hurt the business.

What Else Needs to Go Right?

The methodology described, applied effectively, will result in the desired enterprise-wide risk management architecture. Effective application requires:

- Line management embracing responsibility for risk management. There is a cascading responsibility from the top throughout the organization, with good communication and accountability.
- Facilitation and support to assist line managers.
- A culture that rewards the recognition, communication and management of risks.
- Performance metrics to measure whether business units are taking the right risks to achieve the strategic objectives.
- Human resource performance assessment, compensation and incentive programs linked to managers' risk management performance.

Avoiding a Crisis

Any day, board members could wake to news that something has gone seriously wrong at their company. It could be product tampering, quality problems or manufacturing failures that result in customers or workers being injured, or worse. It could be a rogue trader or price fixing, or sales or compliance issues triggering legal and regulator action. It could be a physical disaster in the company's or a supplier's facility disrupting critical parts of the supply chain. Or it could be a serious shortfall in meeting investors' expectations, or the discovery of misstated financial results.

Companies facing a crisis typically are in a "no win" situation. The media, major investors and regulators are among those asking questions for which there are no ready answers. The company and its management, and sometimes the board, are cast in the worst possible light. The immediate goal becomes damage control, with decisions made in an atmosphere of danger and fear.

Some crises are not reasonably avoidable. But many are. Had the board made sure an effective risk management architecture was in place, the triggering event might never have occurred. With effective risk management systems and related internal controls, risks can be identified and the tremendous losses and corporate and human pain avoided. What's done before a crisis hits is all-important. The board needs to be comfortable that the right risk management processes, including the right communications channels, are in place.

The Opportunity Side of Risk

Business today operates in a new world of speed, complexity and change. Customers might know a company's products only through the click of a mouse, with quickly changing or no allegiance. Competitors' new products come from virtually anywhere on the globe. Industries converge, alliances are disassembled and new ones formed, and supply chains change and compress. All the while, regulators demand attention and shareholders have rigid expectations for performance.

In an environment where everything is moving so fast, standing still is simply not a viable option. Boards of directors and senior executives must continuously move in new strategic directions while pursuing the company's vision and clearly explaining their case to partners, investors, shareholders and sometimes regulators or the courts. And as companies find they must pursue a growth strategy—whether internally or externally driven—the need to identify, measure and monitor upside opportunity increases.

While all companies need an effective risk management architecture, companies in a strong growth mode—and today, which aren't?—must rely most heavily on getting this right. The key is linking strategy, objectives, risk and performance measurement. The more comprehensively and explicitly the company does this, the more assured management and the board will be that the strategic direction chosen is indeed the right one.

Who Has Responsibility?

As noted earlier, line management must accept responsibility for risk management. There are some who argue that line managers need to focus on running the business, and staff functions are best equipped to assume risk management responsibility. Experience shows, and seasoned directors have found, that can be counterproductive.

Where companies have a broad-based view of risk, incorporating all business operations, risk management is both more effective and efficient when line management takes direct responsibility. It's more *effective* because only the line can truly direct human resources within operating activities to do what's necessary to manage risk. Risk exists in all aspects of the business, and the people directly involved are best positioned to identify and deal with it.

It's more *efficient* because risk management is best built into the core activities in a business. When risk management is linked to a business' objectives and strategy, the tasks needed to identify and manage the things that can go wrong and those that must go right are incorporated within the fabric of business and management processes. That way, there's no separate infrastructure superimposed on top of existing business processes.

Why do some companies have separate functions, sometimes called compliance functions, with direct responsibility for risk management? In some cases, such as with broker-dealers, insurance companies, banks and other financial institutions, management deems the risk to be of such nature that a separate compliance function, independent of operating activities, must have this responsibility—either fully or on a shared basis. Financial institution regulators' traditional view of proper risk management supports this approach. In some instances line management has primary responsibility, with a support group verifying that risk management activities are functioning effectively. Typically the support function coordinates its activities with internal audit, together providing senior management and the board with additional comfort.

Companies most recently embracing a risk management architecture place direct responsibility for risk management in the line business unit, with a centralized risk support function. This support group, perhaps led by a "chief risk officer" and typically comprising only a handful of people, provides facilitation skills to assist line managers in building risk management into their business units. The support group provides advice on risk management, and typically has a broad-based monitoring role, here too coordinating with internal audit.

Responsibilities of the key players are set out in Exhibit 2.1.

Exhibit 2.1: Responsibilities for Risk Management

Business Unit Line Managers	Directly responsible for identifying, managing and reporting critical risk issues upstream.
Chief Risk Officer	Acts as line managers' coach, helping them implement a risk management architecture and work with it ongoing. As a member of the senior management team, the CRO monitors the company's entire risk profile, ensuring major risks identified are reported upstream.
Internal Audit	Monitors how well business units manage their risk, in coordination with the CRO. Increasingly, internal audit functions are focusing attention on business units' risk management and control activities, bringing their skills and added value to the business. They also leverage knowledge of the line's risk management architecture in targeting audit activity.
Chief Financial Officer	Handles risk management activities traditionally falling within the CFO's purview, such as treasury and insurance functions. Applies concepts of value-based management and linking risk to value through performance. Some CFOs use models relating shifts in risk factors such as interest rates or commodity prices to movements in share value. Also, acts on behalf of the chief executive spearheading implementation of the risk management architecture. An increasing number of CFOs play a key operating role, and are well positioned to drive their companies to competitive advantage through leading-edge risk management.
Legal Counsel	Typically reports to top management and the board on significant external exposures (from lawsuits, investigations, government inquiries) and internally generated matters (criminal acts, conflicts of interest, employee health and safety issues, harassment). These reports help complete the picture of company risks.
Chief Executive	Brings the power of the CEO office to risk architecture implementation. The CEO needs to support, and be perceived as clearly supporting, the necessary focus on risk management.

Where Responsibility Rests Within the Board

Where within the board should responsibility rest for risk management? Many boards assign that responsibility to the audit committee. Why is that the case? And is that the best place for it?

The "why" is easy. In many boards the primary focus of "risk" historically was reliable *financial reporting*, clearly the realm of the audit committee. In other instances risk has centered on possible failure to *comply with legal and regulatory* requirements, which also might logically fall within the purview of the audit committee. But today's view of risk is much broader, incorporating the activities of every facet of business operation.

A purist's view of where oversight of risk management should lie points to a number of different committees. While financial reporting and certain types of legal and regulatory compliance risk might well be addressed by the audit committee, risks related to strategic issues, marketing and channels, customer care, technology, supply chain and other operational matters might be dealt with by an executive committee or other board subgroup.

That the board effectively discharges this responsibility is more important than where, within the board structure, oversight of risk management resides. What is important, when you cut through it all, is that the board oversees all key risks and ensures a holistic, ongoing risk architecture to identify, manage and monitor risk. Both are extremely important, and both need clearly defined board responsibility and attention.

CHAPTER 3
TONE AT THE TOP

It's not easy to do the right thing all the time. We operate in a world where pressure to effect change quickly and meet aggressive targets is intense. And the pressure is real—if a company fails to meet interim earnings targets or reduces a sales forecast, its stock price can be pummeled. This harsh market reaction, combined with large financial rewards riding on goal achievement, together prove a powerful temptation to stray from the straight and narrow.

Unethical behavior ultimately damages companies and their people. The health care company whose sales force was found culpable of bribing doctors knows this well. So does the investment advisor pushing retirees into high-risk securities and the retailer that was "systematically overcharging" for automotive services. The results? Lost customers, employees and sales, and loss of reputation that took years to build. Some companies never recover.

Avoiding the downside isn't the only reason to worry about ethics. Running a company with consistent integrity and high ethical values is simply good business. Those companies draw the best people and most sought-after customer and supplier relationships, and find open doors to critical alliances, partnerships and merger candidates.

An organization's ethical standards—high or otherwise—spread through the company—from top management through frontline employees. Shared values and goals shape and transform businesses, for better or worse. While the world continues to evolve and businesses face new challenges, dilemmas and technological advances, the need for high ethical standards remains a constant.

Corporate behavior needs to go beyond mere compliance with laws and regulations, which at best is a minimum standard. Most societies expect companies will treat employees, customers and other stakeholders *fairly*. Witness the attention given apparel companies whose products are produced in the third world. While labor practices might meet local standards, that doesn't mean they meet expectations in the developed world.

Why Do Ethical Problems Arise?

The basic values of top management are the main driver. If they're lacking, you can bet that sooner or later values and actions of other personnel will fail. But even where ethical values at the top are sound, inadequate communication can be a major problem. We've seen companies where management never got its expectations about ethical behavior across to employees. In some cases employees didn't bring critical information forward. One survey reports:

- Most employees don't receive the right message from the top, at least when combining managers' actions with their words. While more than 80 percent of CEOs believe they lead by positive personal example, fewer than 40 percent of non-management employees agree.
- Although employees typically know what's going on before a crisis strikes, and 95 percent of CEOs say they have an open door policy and will reward employees who communicate potentially bad news, half of all employees believe the bad news messenger runs a real risk of being seriously damaged.

Even well-intentioned managers striving to do the right thing can send the wrong message. In one example, a financial services business CEO learned that any employee interfacing with customers, to be paid on a commission basis, by law must be licensed—and while the sales force was licensed, customer service personnel weren't. Attempting to do the right thing, the chief executive took swift action, directing immediate steps toward licensing, and moving the service personnel from commission to "straight salary." "To be fair," however, he set a program to adjust salaries each month to equal what commission-based compensation would have been. What message did workers receive? That despite the right words, bottom line compensation hadn't changed, and it was acceptable to keep breaking the law while moving to comply.

Once the wrong signal is sent—inadvertently or not—a mindset permeates a company. Employees believe it's acceptable to "work around" other legal and ethical challenges. A number of companies learned a bitter lesson when unacceptable ethical values entered the corporate culture and were allowed to fester. How does this happen? Toxic environments are created when monetary or other incentives for making the numbers are overwhelming, or the punishment for missing them, such as public peer ridicule or job termination, is extreme. Combine the reward/penalty factors with lack of sensitivity to feedback on difficult business issues, and people begin feeling they have little choice. A "no excuses" senior management mentality often leads to bad behavior, like earnings manipulation or production "shortcuts."

What Should Management Be Doing?

Effective boards recognize that corporate culture starts first and foremost with the tone set by corporate leadership—top management. The "tone at the top" establishes the true expectation for behavior. And the right behavior must be practiced consistently by management—through good times and bad.

Indeed, behavior in bad times, or when crisis hits, sends the most powerful signal of all. Conversely, a well-established culture, formed over years and applied consistently, will drive management's behavior in time of crisis, just when direction is most needed and time to carefully debate and consider myriad options is limited. In the oft-cited Tylenol product-tampering crisis, consensus exists among observers that management did exactly the right thing, although less attention is given to why that happened. There are many reasons, some of which likely are not known beyond the individuals directly involved. But one important reason is the company's culture for dealing with stakeholders. Encompassed in its mission statement and nurtured and applied over many years, the culture set a clear path for dealing with the crisis. The only answer the culture allowed was to immediately pull product from store shelves, and the rest is history. Some observers contrast this example with that in the tobacco industry, with assertions of deception coupled with intense public scrutiny and damaging litigation.

How does a company develop the desired value-based culture? We know it starts with the mindset and actions of the chief executive and senior management team. Beyond that there are basic steps that facilitate and foster a culture that permeates an organization. This begins with selectively recruiting people with track records of performance and values consistent with the company's, and reinforcing appropriate behavior through effective human resources practices, including remuneration. Other basics include:

- *Code of conduct.* A written code of conduct is an important plank supporting the corporate culture—a foundation document. All levels of management must not only adhere to the code, but also be seen as adhering to it. A survey shows that when faced with an ethical dilemma, employees do what their supervisors expect, even when that action doesn't comply with company ethics policy. Exhibit 3.1 summarizes key elements one might expect to see in such a code.
- *Communicating expectations.* Management needs to be sure people are knowledgeable about the code and know the penalties for violations. Not only should the code be readily available (through company intranets or on bulletin boards), but periodic communications (through newsletters, intranets, posters) should reinforce its importance and relevance.
- *Available channels.* Leading companies have long known the importance of providing supplemental communication channels through which personnel can get help when dealing with troublesome ethics issues. Circumstances arise when an individual just doesn't feel comfortable reporting issues directly to his/her manager, or where that individual might be seen as part of the problem. Hotlines or ombudspersons are used, staffed in some cases by legal counsel or a compliance office.
- *Explicit accountability.* Companies have learned that requiring personnel to confirm in writing they've read the code and are in compliance refreshes knowledge, reinforces expectations and positively affects actual compliance. It also allows investigation of reported suspected violations.
- *Investigation and Enforcement.* It's critical that issues are investigated carefully and infractions handled consistently—regardless of the status of the individual involved. The

easiest way to undermine corporate values is to let the top salesperson get away with actions—like expense account padding or harassment—that would result in dismissal for other employees.

- *Communicating results*. Ethics violations need to be tracked and reported to senior levels. Types of violations and source—by business unit, geography or other categorization—should be identified. Summaries of issues and their resolutions should be communicated to staff, reinforcing that they are taken seriously.

Leading companies now self-assess their ethical standards, the same way they might assess supply chain or other process effectiveness. Nonattribution surveys asking employees about their experiences, including the example they see management setting, can be useful. Results can point to omissions in training or communications programs and surface issues local management might have suppressed. Done well, surveys provide an effective outlet for staff to report contentious practices with which they're not comfortable but feel insufficiently powerful to contest.

One might expect to see an ethics officer in the above list. Some companies make effective use of this role, serving as an enabler for policy and process, and a monitor and centralized focal point for information on potential violations. But experience shows that while an ethics office can be useful, often it is a double-edged sword. Despite instruction to the contrary, managers can fall into the trap of believing the office has *responsibility* for effecting compliance with the code of conduct.

A foundation principle is that, to be most effective, line management must accept responsibility and be held accountable for living the corporate values, including maintaining ethical standards. Management's actions drive behavior, and managers are responsible for establishing the right environment and knowing what's going on within their spheres of responsibility. And they are uniquely positioned to act on information that surfaces. It's true that support staff can be serve a purpose for busy executives, but nothing should get in the way of making it absolutely clear to all where responsibility and accountability lie. This point cannot be overemphasized. When responsibility—real or assumed—rests anyplace other than with line management, problems are more likely to occur and go unnoticed or untreated.

While the right management processes need to be in place for the reasons discussed, laws in some countries provide further impetus. A particularly relevant law in the United States is the Federal Sentencing Guidelines. The law applies to all companies doing business in the United States, whether incorporated in the U.S. or not. With a properly implemented, effective compliance program, a company found to have acted illegally benefits with reduced fines and penalties. Ensuring compliance is a clear way for directors to protect shareholder value, given the likelihood some employee, somewhere in an organization, someday is bound to break a law.

Exhibit 3.1: Ethics Policy Topics

- Employee and customer privacy
- Workplace safety and violence
- Environmental protection
- Conflicts of interest, including family and personal relationships, outside employment and financial investments
- Dealing with the media
- Political contributions
- Protecting company assets
- Intellectual property and trade secrets
- Confidential information
- Computer data and security
- Industrial espionage
- Protecting company funds and accurately reporting company information
- Gifts, entertainment and gratuities
- Equal employment opportunity and non-discrimination
- Global business practices, including coverage of Foreign Corrupt Practices Act, import/export regulations, anti-boycott laws, applicable local laws and regulations, and other applicable industry laws and regulations
- Fair competition, anti-competitive laws and gathering and using competitive data
- Sexual harassment
- Relationships with vendors, suppliers, contractors, joint venture partners and other third parties
- Relationships with customers
- Product quality and safety, including consumer protection standards
- Advertising and marketing practices
- Insider trading

How Does the Board Know?

Effective directors recognize that a key part of management's job is to instill a positive ethical culture, and the board needs to get a handle on how well management is doing this. This isn't just a good idea—directors are fully expected to make sure the company's culture is sound, and to monitor ethics, values and compliance with laws and policies. Indeed, the precedent-setting Caremark case in the United States established directors' duty to assure that their companies have an effective compliance and reporting system.

How can directors judge corporate culture for themselves? The best boards know it's not enough to read the code of conduct. They recognize they need to get behind the verbiage and know what's going on. "I always had a good notion, based on my understanding of the tone at the top, whether the CEO was leveling with the board and getting along with executives," says one director. As a starting point, directors like him obtain information on:

- The de facto corporate culture that management has established, for themselves and for all other employees.
- Areas of greatest ethics/compliance-related risk to the company.

- Nature of the violations that arise or concerns reported to hot lines, for example pressure to cut corners or to ignore government regulations. The board agrees on a threshold with management, beyond which issues are considered to be of such a serious nature that they require immediate reporting.
- Extent to which violations are dealt with consistently.
- Results of ethical standards assessments periodically carried out.

Going beyond this start is critical. Experienced directors have a variety of means of getting their arms around the real culture:

- Probably most important, and emphasized by many knowledgeable directors, is direct contact with people throughout the company, allowing the director to make his or her own assessment. Store, branch and factory floor visits—"going to the coal face"—enable a director to see how messages from the top are received and interpreted downstream. Middle management is where most of the filtering occurs, and negative responses from these individuals can indicate big problems within the company. Savvy directors use these visits to determine what attitudes and morals are espoused by managers and how they're embraced by the rank and file.
- Also essential is direct contact with customers. Are they happy with the company's products or services? Were their questions answered? If they had a problem, how well was it resolved? Do they recommend the company to their colleagues and friends?
- Supplier input is also sought. Were agreements adhered to? Were suppliers paid promptly? Are they planning to renew their contract?

Directors monitor other indicators—high executive turnover, for one—that may indicate whether a productive environment exists at the company. One director doing so found that "the CEO had no respect for ethical principles. He basically got ahead over the strewn bodies of associates." Another indicator is the extent of pending and threatened litigation—from customers, employees, suppliers and government agencies—that can indicate the company's approach to dealing with stakeholders.

If directors find the tone at the top is lacking, it's up to the board to provide requisite coaching to management. It's absolutely essential that the manager accepts that a problem exists and is open to board suggestions. If not, more drastic action may be needed.

Ethics in Times of Change

When considering a business combination, effective boards quickly home in on culture issues. Before and during the due diligence process, the best boards are certain to understand enough about both companies' culture, including ethical values, to determine whether the deal makes sense. Cultural issues usually aren't the first areas of focus, with scale, process, products, channels, technology and other synergies first on the radar screen. But cultural issues can make or break a deal—if not up front, then after the fact. Also important, although surprisingly often not addressed early, is basic honesty. More than a few companies found themselves in bed with cheats and liars. In one case, only post-merger did the dominant merger partner realize that its partner's highly personable CEO was booking fictitious revenues, dictating to subsidiaries what numbers they had to report. The resulting restatement wiped out close to 75 percent of the prior three years' earnings.

Beyond uncovering ethical problems, management needs to decide how best to integrate the cultures. Why? Experience shows unless high-level attention is given, the combined company's ethical values find the *lowest* common denominator. As the joint workforce begins working together, unless they receive clear direction, they'll invariably take the quickest and easiest way to do things—and that way won't necessarily be consistent with the culture of either predecessor company. Directors experienced with mergers know the best result is when neither company's culture is allowed to dominate. They want, instead, a weaving of the best of both cultures. This is accomplished by analyzing similarities and differences—and not glossing over the differences, which may be caused by global locations, types of business or maturity of the companies' model or products.

There are instances where an acquirer decides to shield an acquired company, wanting to retain the target's special cultural qualities. One well-known case is the large computer manufacturer that, when buying a software company, set a clear objective of not imposing its then bureaucratic culture, fearing it might stifle creativity—a key asset it was paying for.

Meaningful board involvement really is crucial. In bringing together two companies, management is dealing with so many other challenges that if the board isn't involved, these critical cultural issues might be ignored.

And it's not just mergers that present problems. Monitoring ethics in a rapidly growing industry can be difficult, and here directors need to be particularly vigilant. Especially for companies in their infancy or entering new businesses, markets or channels, the need for speed is overwhelming—to be first with product, to capture quickly emerging customers and markets, and to seize the high ground as sales and order fulfillment channel opportunities suddenly emerge. Reality is that little attention is given to practices that will support or haunt the company into the future. For instance, with e-commerce catching fire, directors of the dot-coms need to make sure consumers are satisfied and compliance issues addressed. Customers who get a great price but don't receive the merchandise likely are lost forever. What happens if customers' credit card information is stolen and posted to other Web sites? If a company's culture allows unfair treatment, customers instantly will take their money elsewhere.

Ethical Behavior at the Board Level

Directors themselves have ethical obligations to the company and to one another. How a board tackles its own ethical issues sends a very clear signal to the CEO and senior management, and ultimately throughout the company.

The best boards look at the independence of their individual members, considering circumstances that might inadvertently or otherwise have an impact on the ability to make decisions in the very best interest of the company. They consider, for example, the director who has a special supplier relationship, or could benefit even indirectly from a specific transaction, and fully expect the individual to remove him- or herself from related decisions. What about the director whose board seat represents a venture capitalist whose primary focus might be protecting the needs of one individual or a specific group rather than equally representing all shareholders? Similar issues might exist with directors with other significant business relationships with the company, or where compensation committee links exist with other boards. And such relationships with close family members also can pose potential conflicts.

An experienced observer makes the point that, " . . . in reality, what is really needed is a spirit of independence, with freedom from conflicts of interest and a willingness to question. The written definitions usually fall short."

Beyond director objectivity is how the board as a whole and directors individually deal with business issues that surface. What ethical values are brought to bear, or ignored for the sake of expediency? How the board handles the most pressing, threatening and challenging problems is perhaps the most direct indicator of the corporate culture. Those board actions will have the most direct impact on the values embraced and brought to bear by management and ultimately every employee throughout the organization.

What does a board member do if uncomfortable with the ethical values practiced? One director lays out a clear roadmap: "If I became aware of a serious ethical situation with any board member, including the chair, I'd first address the issue with that individual. If he or she refused to either rectify the issue or resign, I'd report the issue to the chair and all other directors, and if they didn't take action, I'll resign my seat—I see no other choice."

CHAPTER 4 MEASURING AND MONITORING PERFORMANCE

A past mayor of New York City routinely stopped his constituents on the street, asking "How'm I doin'?" This began immediately after the election and continued throughout his term. Make that *terms*. He was reelected again and again.

Monitoring company performance must be done right and continuously. Done well, it allows a board to really know to what extent management is successfully implementing the approved strategy and operating plans. But to do so properly, the board needs to move well beyond reviewing traditional financial reports. Industries, markets and competitors have become too complicated and dynamic for these measures alone. And financial measures are largely after-the-fact yardsticks. Effective directors are skilled in identifying and using predictors of future performance, not merely evaluating what has already happened. And they recognize that performance measures that may have been used in the past won't work for the future if the measures don't directly link to shareholder value.

Experience shows that many boards have not had success knowing what to look for. Witness the number of companies with poor performance, or worse. Boards can fail because it is difficult to interpret signs of impending trouble and to find the courage to act decisively. If they wait for solid evidence of failing performance, it's probably too late, with the damage already done. Many times individual directors have concerns about performance but are reluctant to speak up—not wanting to be seen as another Chicken Little. We've seen this particularly in large boards with unspoken pressure to keep to a highly structured meeting agenda. As one experienced director noted, "Not enough boards pay attention to their gut feeling when something is not right. They need to have the courage to probe and get to the heart of what is bothering them and not ignore their intuition."

The Movement to Measure

As more companies reexamine their performance measures, the measures are found lacking. Some managements have corrected deficiencies with minor additions and shifts, while others find a need to essentially scrap what's there and develop a new set of measures from scratch. Why the increased focus on measurement? Managements and directors point to a desire to:

- Improve targeted unit, process and company-wide performance.
- Sharpen employees' and management's focus on common objectives and tactics.
- Identify and turn around suboptimal performance.
- Effectively motivate employees, rewarding them for achieving the right goals.
- Properly integrate merged or acquired companies.

Why Is Evaluating Performance So Difficult?

With the importance of effective measures widely recognized, and significant resources devoted to upgrading information systems, why are measurement metrics lacking? Too often measures:

- Don't clearly link to the company's strategy.
- Are calculated in business silos and don't provide performance data on cross-unit business results or a company-wide picture.
- Aren't benchmarked against peers, competitors or industry players. This is a particularly important issue for high-tech and other companies where innovations quickly change the competitive landscape, and velocity and convergence create new products, channels and even industries overnight.

Measures used in some companies don't allow management to truly assess company performance. This might be for the simple reason that relevant information just isn't available. And if management doesn't have it, it's a safe bet that the board doesn't either. One director recounted an incident where in a two-year period the company completed 24 acquisitions. Requesting monthly revenue reports for the acquired companies, she was told they didn't exist. Management finally dug out reports showing 19 of the companies had declining revenues within three months of acquisition, indicating "the acquisitions were mismanaged, the company had overpaid, or both." Ultimately, the board felt compelled to replace the CEO, who had founded the company and driven the acquisitions.

How Leading Companies Measure

Before a board can properly evaluate corporate performance, management needs to have identified the right set of measures—featuring nonfinancial indicators as well as financial ones. What are the right measures? The answer lies in the linkage of value drivers—shareholder value growth factors—to measures. Exhibit 4.1 shows an example of this linkage.

While understanding what drives value might seem like a given, more than one-third of top executives said their companies don't identify value drivers effectively. The frequent result is that measures are set without assurance that their achievement will get shareholder value where it needs to be.

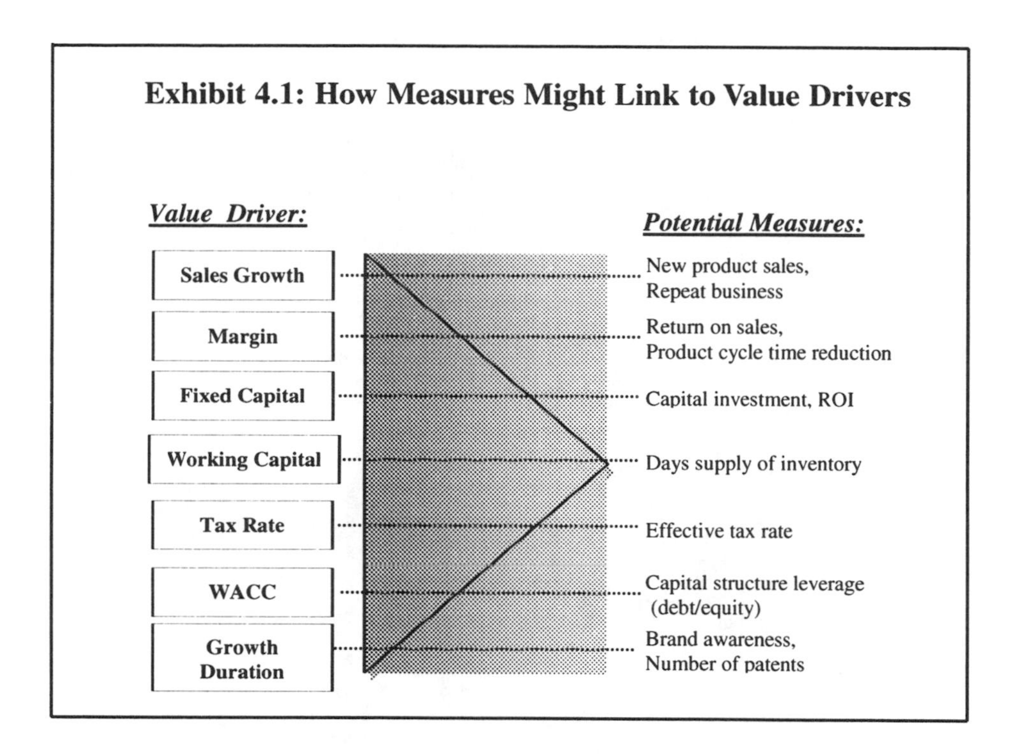

The right set of measures will have good balance between leading and lagging indicators—something that's proven difficult to achieve. Lagging indicators describe where the company has been and include traditional measures, such as return on equity. These, used alone, are not timely enough to guide management in correcting performance. Leading indicators serve as an early signal for future performance successes or problems.

Through measures like customer and employee satisfaction, a company not only can develop a predictive capability, but also can drill down into causative factors and finer measures. For instance, a company tracking the rate of employee departures should be positioned to know whether an increase results from ineffective management processes or competitors luring them away with different or better compensation programs.

How does a board know whether management has set the right measures—those with enough leading indicators linked to shareholder value growth? By looking first at the process used in their development and their linkage to the company's strategy, tactics and actions flowing from the risk management process. This is depicted by a simple example, shown in Exhibit 4.2.

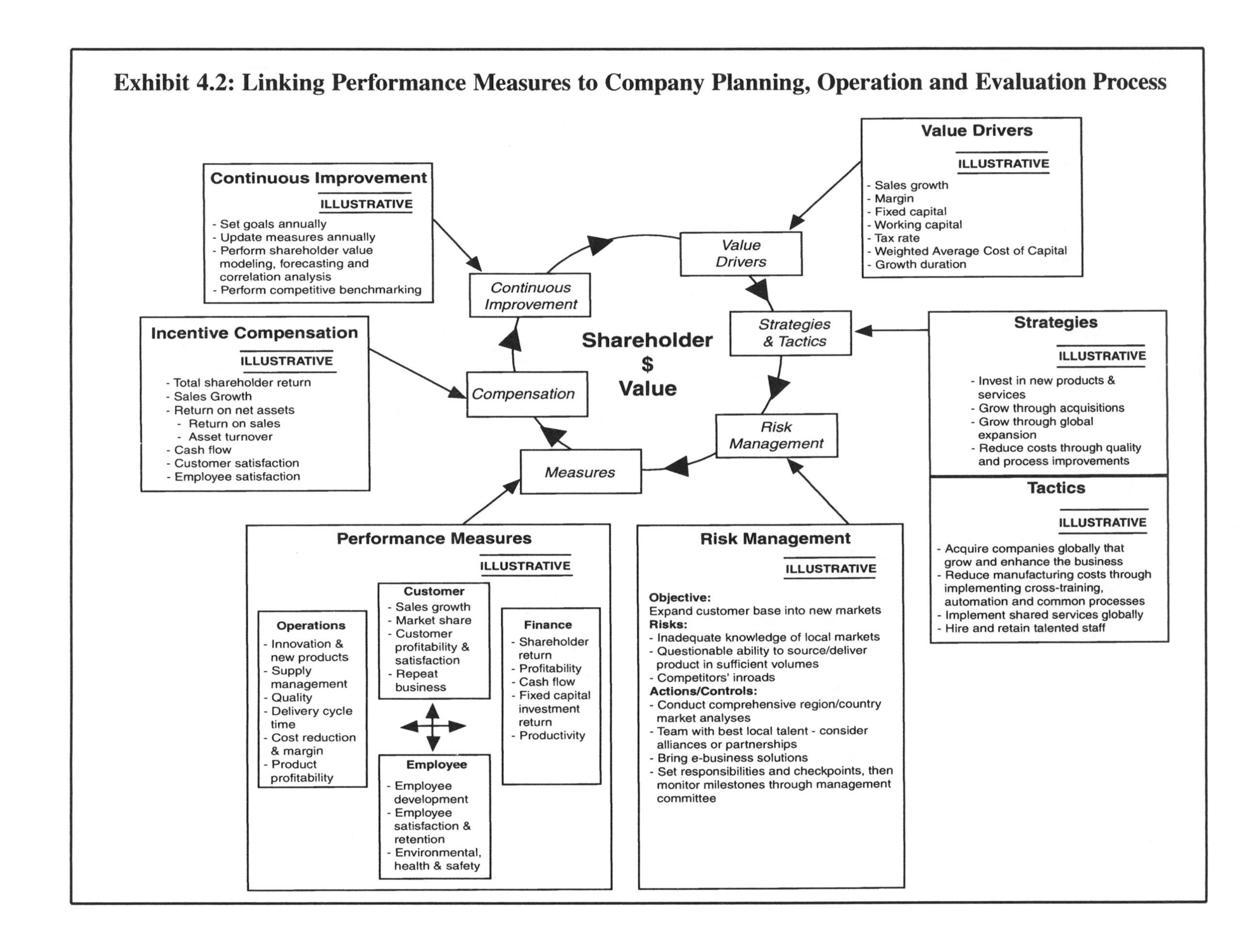

Exhibit 4.2: Linking Performance Measures to Company Planning, Operation and Evaluation Process

The Exhibit illustrates companies' need to:

- Create clear links between performance measures and shareholder value—a task many companies find difficult as they struggle with measuring intangibles, such as the value derived from research and development or the lifetime value of customers.
- Lock performance measures into strategy—to show the real progress made in achieving strategy.
- Ensure decision making and business processes at each level of the company are linked to the strategy, with middle management buy-in.
- Link measures and targets to recognition and reward processes, thereby driving the right values and behaviors.
- Fully support the measurement process with robust information systems, which deliver the right information to the right place at the right time.

The process is conceptually straightforward, but must be grounded in having a great strategy, the right linkage and developing measures that are truly meaningful and relevant within the context of the company's industry, culture and processes. Much thought and effort are needed to get this right. Too many companies have tracked the wrong measures, without the requisite predictive relationships, only to find too late that shareholder value was being eroded rather than enhanced.

The performance measures depicted above incorporate a balanced scorecard concept, with a shared focus on measures in a number of categories. Purposefully keeping categories and measures to a limited number forces management to identify the most important. Avoiding a temptation to measure anything that moves helps both management and the board focus on a workable set.

Leading companies are including their key intangibles within the sights of performance measures. While these can be extremely difficult to get a handle on, they're becoming increasingly important in the evolution of measuring what's important. When one thinks for a moment about intangibles like intellectual capital, brand effectiveness, customer base, e-business-based distribution channels and innovation, it quickly becomes apparent that good measures are critical.

Pulling It Together

What, then, should directors look for in their companies' performance measures? Exhibit 4.3 summarizes the key steps in a measurement-setting process and requisite elements of effective measurement sets.

Exhibit 4.3: Core Principles Underlying Effective Performance Measurement

Link Measurements to Value Drivers, Strategies and Tactics:	• Key drivers of shareholder value need to be clearly defined and understood • Measures should support and link to the drivers of shareholder value • Measures should be derived from and directly linked to strategies and tactics and should be amended when strategies change
Balance Measurements Across Scorecard and Key Processes:	• Measurement sets should be balanced across the key scorecard categories such as operations, customer, employee and finance/shareholder • Measurement sets should be balanced across the key value chain processes for the company
Balance Measurement Viewpoint:	• Measurement sets should highlight predictive, process-oriented measures as well as results-oriented measures (leading and lagging) • Measurement sets should be both internally and externally focused
Use a Reliable Measurement Selection Process:	• A small set of measures should be selected using a structured approach that builds consensus • Measures should be easy to understand, linked to strategies and support current business processes • Appropriate measures should be selected for each level of the organization
Set and Monitor Goals:	• Quantifiable goals or targets should be set for all measurements at least annually • Progress toward achieving goals should be assessed and commented on regularly • Measures should be externally benchmarked wherever possible
Ensure Consistent Measurement and Reporting:	• Measures should use consistent definitions across locations or groups • Reports should be formatted using consistent organizational dimensions (e.g., function, geography), presentation, level of detail and time periods
Automate Measurement and Reporting:	• Measures and reports should be automated and should support drill down and aggregation capabilities • Data warehousing and data mining alternatives should be utilized where appropriate for reporting measures and performing detailed cause and effect analysis • Shareholder value modeling should be performed to determine optimal performance alternatives • Systems should highlight control limits and exception reporting where possible
Link Measurement to Compensation:	• Measures that support the key drivers of value and strategies should be linked to the compensation system for a wide range of employees • Compensation programs should emphasize both unit and overall company performance

Accessing and Using Information

Effective boards know they need to make sure that:

- Management is getting the right information and using it effectively in proactively monitoring performance.
- Directors are getting information they need to oversee what's going on.

Directors traditionally have received the bulk of their information from management. That makes sense, because management is in the best position to accumulate and analyze data and shape it into information most meaningful to the board level. Increasingly, however, directors supplement that information through other sources.

Experienced directors know the value of being in touch with employees and customers directly, to corroborate information received through traditional sources or to balance it with other viewpoints. This is one way to check that information coming to the board isn't overly filtered of bad news. A director of an Australian-based wood fiber carton manufacturer, on a tour of European countries, observed that an unusually large number of customers were using plastic crates, a threat management hadn't identified for the board. Armed with this firsthand knowledge, the director was better positioned to discuss the strategic implications with the board and management. Another director who sits on the boards of a major retailer and manufacturer espouses the importance of getting "out there." He's found circumstances where what is said "at the factory or store level" as happening is very different from the direction in which management wanted to go.

Critical in measuring performance is the ability of information systems and processes to accumulate relevant data and deliver it to management. For years now companies have turned to sophisticated, integrated enterprise resource planning (ERP) systems. Among the better known are PeopleSoft, SAP, and Oracle, which when effectively implemented can gather and make available extremely useful performance data.

Importantly, directors themselves are gaining direct access to such information. Corporate intranets are allowing directors to stay in touch and exchange information on operational successes and difficulties. Minutes of departmental meetings and brainstorming sessions are posted. One director emphasized how being "on-line" allows him to access all the information he needs. He reviews basic financial information, progressively drilling down for greater detail—an opportunity not previously available. A number of directors said they're much more knowledgeable of what's going on because they see the information management uses, before screening or filtering.

Directors have reported instances where management simply refuses to share information. It's evident, although perhaps worth repeating, that if a director believes the board is not being provided information it needs to make informed judgments, and management is unwilling to provide it, extreme remedial action likely is needed.

Directors shouldn't assume all information they receive, through reports or directly by accessing systems, is always accurate. The risk exists that management or employees made honest errors in compiling and calculating data, or intentionally provided overly optimistic (or even downright fraudulent) results. Directors need to apply common sense and ask questions on information sources and analyze information in the context of their knowledge base and experience with the company.

Given the Daunting Challenges, What Is a Director to Do?

Directors can use their understanding of how the leading companies measure performance and their recognition of the attendant difficulties to positively influence the performance measurement process. What's the best way to do this?

- Find out whether the principles outlined above are used in developing performance measures, linking value drivers, strategy, tactics, measures and rewards. Don't nit-pick at the detail, but rather think strategically.
- Make sure performance measures are consistent with the desired corporate culture. An often-quoted saying is, "You get what you measure." The way measures are designed will knowingly or otherwise encourage a set of values and behaviors.
- Agree early with management on the financial and nonfinancial information that will serve as fundamental performance measurements, and concur on targets or ranges.
- Ensure management has robust processes in place, along with effective controls, so the board is comfortable with information reliability.
- Review reported metrics carefully and timely. Effective monitoring, with a sharp focus on leading indicators, enables board determination of the extent to which management is on track or should initiate corrective action.
- Fully discuss reasons for missed targets—whether performance falls short or overshoots. (Significantly overshooting a target might signal taking on too much risk or setting too low a target, or perhaps something very positive.) Watch for targets being changed in midstream, or shortfalls explained away without justification. While directors understand the need for flexibility, some boards continually allow repeatedly missed targets to go without needed action.

Effectively implementing these guidelines is a balancing act. On the one hand, directors want the company to meet performance targets. On the other, they don't want targets set so conservatively that hitting them is virtually assured. Stretch goals are useful, but management shouldn't be held accountable for missing too much of a "stretch"—setting a bar too high can be a disincentive.

A number of directors have indicated they feel uneasy when addressing missed targets with management. Discomfort is much more likely when directors didn't clearly communicate expectations to management up front. Serious problems also have occurred when the board isn't apprised early on when targets are in danger of being missed. It's critical that the board is told immediately. Simply put by an experienced director, "Executives need to get bad news on the table, and get it on the table early." But directors need to make sure they're not perceived by management as just waiting to find fault. Rather, they need to promote a climate that encourages management to readily approach both the full board and individual directors for counsel.

CHAPTER 5 TRANSFORMATIONAL TRANSACTIONS

News Flash: Most Acquisitions Reduce Shareholder Value!

Virtually all recent studies on acquisitions conclusively confirm that the vast majority of acquisitions fail to meet acquirers' objectives. Many never recover the purchase price, let alone the cost of capital.

While acquisitions are typically an enterprise's biggest bet, relatively few companies have an unblemished acquisitions record. And even the most sophisticated acquirers believe they can do better. With all these chips on the table, what can a board do to ensure shareholders' interests are protected and value maximized—that the bet will pay off?

Directors experienced in the world of acquirers have come to recognize certain realities:

- Access to target information is severely limited.
- The limited timeframe available for negotiations and due diligence, from start to close, challenges the bounds of common sense.
- The price paid for the target will be greater than its market value (current market capitalization).

These facts of life, resulting in part from the narcotic effect of closing the deal on senior management and the investment bankers, dramatically increase the risk that a company will pay more than the target is worth.

Chances of success in acquisitions are tentative at best for additional reasons. In all but a narrow set of tactical acquisitions, companies pay a value today that will be realized only by effectively implementing significant change in an unforgiving environment of competitor reaction, loss of key managers, customer reactions and changing markets, to name a few. And, public and often nonpublic information available in the due diligence process is insufficient to confirm important financial and operating assumptions and build effective implementation plans—with many acquirers essentially rolling the dice only to find critical assumptions were erroneous.

Successfully executing a strategy with flawed detailed assumptions makes roulette odds seem attractive, even more so when the solution is an acquisition. A common scapegoat for poor execution of the transaction and subsequent integration is the claim that the company paid too much, but history irrefutably demonstrates that paying too much is the effect—rarely the cause.

Savvy directors look closely at their team. If they have serious reservations about the team's ability—encompassing management and external support—to effectuate critically needed change, they have similarly serious reservations about moving forward with an acquisition.

Merger and acquisition strategies inherently have a high degree of risk. Within the context of M&A strategies, it is useful to segregate risks, and match them with the level of board oversight. Exhibit 5.1 shows the risk matrix.

Exhibit 5.1: Level of Relative Acquisition Risk

Target is in:	Same Business	Related Business	Unrelated Business
Same Countries	Low	Medium	High
New Countries	Medium	High	Very High

Other factors to consider in setting the level of board involvement are the size of the investment (near and long term), visibility in the marketplace and targets with special relationships such as a significant customer or affiliate.

Looking at underlying problems inherent in the M&A arena, we find common fault lines underlying the following three factors. Directors experienced in looking at potential acquisitions deal with each head on.

1: Flawed or Unfocused Strategy

Acquisitions often are accompanied by or the intended vehicle for implementing laudable strategies such as increasing market share, obtaining critical mass, establishing a cross-border growth platform, extending or globalizing a brand, coping with convergence, acquiring new capabilities and diversification. But without sufficiently understanding the financial implications of successful execution, and having a realistic plan to capture the value, the probability of failure increases.

What do effective boards do to decrease the probability of failure? They:

- Make sure they get real market and competitor research and facts, and critically assess underlying strategic and market assumptions.
- Look at available internal and external management and support expertise with a critical eye.
- Ensure the planned acquisition plays to the enterprise's competencies, or will bring truly new ones.
- Analyze critical risks and opportunities presented by different economic and competitive scenarios, and map target strategies and tactics to these scenarios. They consider whether operating flexibility will be enhanced or limited following target company integration, taking advantage of advanced analytical tools such as simulations and real options analysis.
- Monitor the corporate development group's activities, avoiding surprises.
- Make sure the target would help the company advance a focused strategy. They ask: Why this target versus others? Is acquisition cheaper than a "greenfield" program (growing capabilities internally from scratch)?

As the enterprise goes further from its primary markets, failure risk increases. Effective boards mitigate the higher risk by more rigorous use of subject matter and market experts and thorough investigative efforts.

2: Inadequate Due Diligence

What is your company's acquisition reputation in the market? Companies looked upon as sophisticated acquirers often walk away from a bad deal and closely guard their reputation for follow-through—and as a result tend to pay less or get better terms on the deals they close.

Due diligence failures tend to fall into one or more of four categories:

- Insufficient information
- Inexperienced team members
- Flawed communication and coordination
- Poor preclose follow-up and integration planning

By contrast, successful acquirers have a well-coordinated process—between the deal team and subject matter experts in market analysis, operations, technology, finance, human resources, treasury and legal—and utilize experienced acquisition teams with a team manager who has accountability. They are certain to obtain sufficient detailed operational and financial information to substantiate anticipated synergies and base line run rates, and continually update information in the period before closing, with particular emphasis on planning early integration actions that drive value. And they utilize knowledge and skills of internal or external auditors to validate critical information as necessary.

Examples abound of financial disasters resulting from a failed due diligence process. One Fortune 500 acquirer closed on a multibillion dollar transaction with another public company in a converging industry with no detailed financial and operating due diligence—arguing that the target's public information was sufficient. The deal backfired, helping solidify this acquirer's acquisition record as among the worst in recent decades.

Directors who want to ensure their company performs effective due diligence understand the full extent of the due diligence process and see that significant issues raised are adequately dealt with. They are up to speed with and closely monitor the process.

These directors also ascertain whether operating personnel believe they can deliver the synergies and make good the assumptions in the valuation model. The best boards ask the question: Is management prepared to have its bonuses dependent on delivery of the synergies—both cost and growth? It's true that the board can remove senior managers that don't deliver, but by that time it's already too late, with significant shareholder value already lost. Boards need to make sure management gets it right the first time!

3: Flawed Post-Deal Integration

Premiums required to successfully close a deal in today's marketplace can be justified only if deal synergies are swiftly and efficiently captured. Speed and focus on actions that quickly create shareholder value are critical. There is little or no value in a prolonged transition.

Some of the common pitfalls of merger transition include:

- Creating never-ending "to do" lists and forming numerous oversized teams to plan the transition. This behavior leads to dilution of resources and slows progress.
- Failing to address the needs and concerns of key stakeholders, especially customers and employees. Post-deal communications tend to continue promoting the transaction without regard to these stakeholders, keeping them in a state of confusion.
- Making management decisions about authority, control and reporting structure based on form over function, titles over accountability, or some type of democratic quota system. Companies often become preoccupied with organization charts.
- Believing that cultures can be merged gradually through contact and interaction, by proclaiming shared vision and values. Integrating two cultures requires hard work aligning two distinct sets of behavior.

The best boards add great value at this stage by:

- Carefully reviewing the integration plan. The board ensures management gives top priority to taking actions that will drive economic and shareholder value in the shortest timeframe

with the greatest probability of success. All available resources are allocated first to these value-creating priorities so as to capture early wins and create momentum.
- Focusing on integration communication and compensation plans, making sure they address the needs and concerns of all significant stakeholders. Open communications addressing stakeholder issues will keep stakeholders focused and energized—that is, producing, buying or investing. And by controlling the communications environment, an organization is much less likely to be victimized by it.
- Seeing that key management roles and relationships are clearly defined based on business values, and that organization structure decisions are made not on a political basis but on the basis of skill sets and operating style. The board makes sure the new management team fully understands the different cultures and creates a desired behavior pattern that will support the combined business' strategies and values.

Even previously effective management teams can be stretched by acquisitions. Endless detail and complex issues overwhelm some managers, while others put themselves far above it all, making it impossible to appreciate the complexity. An effective board anticipates these likely possibilities and works with management to avoid these sometimes-fatal pitfalls.

Divestitures – the Flip Side of the Coin

Most sophisticated companies periodically reassess the strategic value of all portions of the enterprise. Outside forces such as an unsolicited offer or competitor acquisition that change the landscape may be the impetus for a reassessment. When internal or external forces suggest a portion or all of the enterprise has a higher and better use in someone else's hands, the divestiture process requires special care by the board.

The sale of a business creates wealth transfers, for or at the expense of the selling shareholders. Balancing the interests of shareholders with other stakeholders, particularly employees who are affected by the divestiture, can be tricky.

Legal issues exist pertaining to fairness of price for dispositions and addressing management conflicts, for example, as a result of compensation programs affected by a deal or poison pill. A company's general counsel supported by outside counsel represent key support to a board in dealing with its legal/fiduciary responsibilities.

Notwithstanding the differing legal obligations, shareholder rights and business practices that tend to vary by geography, a potential business sale creates biases that the board must address. In doing so, directors should:

- Recognize that managers in the unit being sold may have more to gain in the event a sale is consummated than if not. Their benefit might even depend on to whom it is sold. Managers faced with these inherent conflicts need to be insulated from final decision making.

- Understand the value of the business to the organization and to whom the business is most valuable, before initiating the process of hiring an investment banker.
- Consider the fact that if investment bankers are engaged to lead the sale, the fee arrangement is attractive only if a sale occurs. Thus, their financial interests are focused primarily on obtaining the sale mandate and somewhat less so on achieving the greatest value, particularly at the risk of no sale. On a $1 billion sale, for example, an investment banker might be relatively indifferent to a $100 million swing in price either way. It might be better to involve in negotiations a party whose primary interest is value maximization over the long term.
- Recognize when the price is inadequate. In such cases directors must have the courage to stop the process and employ alternative strategies to achieve value. Board support for or initiation of such brave decisions can be crucial.
- Take personnel actions to preserve and maximize sale value, such as management contracts for key people and special compensation programs like stay bonuses. The evaluation must consider that an acquirer might not intend to keep all employees, but also recognize that how the organization treats exiting personnel will affect relations with remaining employees. Severance programs can be crafted to balance conflicting objectives. Because some time after the sale announcement but before the close employees' allegiance changes, it's important to act to protect the company's interest during this process. One technique involves temporarily placing a company manager in the unit being sold to facilitate integration planning with the buyer in a way that ensures the selling company is protected.

As with the sale of a unit, this same level of care must be brought to selling licenses or outsourcing critical functions. Too often, these transactions are effected without sound focus on corporate strategy or value preservation. In one case, for example, an executive negotiated the long-term outsourcing of his company's selling function for a significant geographic market segment. While it reaped a large up-front payment that allowed the company to make budget, the enterprise essentially mortgaged its future by severely limiting the economic value of its sales channels for key products and services. In the end, the company paid dearly to buy out the contract.

Alliances and Joint Ventures – Other Value-Building Tools

Increasingly, businesses that wish to expand their product line, customer base or geographic reach are turning to alliances or joint ventures in lieu of acquisitions. Joint ventures—to which companies contribute assets—often are used to strengthen research and development or streamline a company's supply chain. Alliances—most other arrangements fit under this umbrella—are increasingly prevalent between technology companies and marketing companies to build customer base. The contributing partners' individual needs drive which type of venture is appropriate for them. Exhibit 5.2 is a partial list of drivers and the related types of suitable ventures.

Exhibit 5.2: Selecting the Appropriate Transaction

Value Drivers	Potential Joint Venture Types
Access to customer base/geographic region	Distribution arrangement
Utilization of excess capacity	Subcontract
Access to patent/technology/R&D	License agreement, Subcontract
Access to skilled workforce	Subcontract

For significant transactions, sophisticated directors monitor a variety of issues: the strategic objective/value drivers, the existence of alternative structures, access to capital investment, partner competencies, communication and venture integration. Key concerns fall into three interrelated categories:

- Choosing the right partner
- Structuring the deal
- Due diligence

The Partner

Once directors accept that an alliance of some type makes sense, they need to understand the value the potential partner brings to the deal. Based on its due diligence, management should be able to discuss with the board:

- The partner's strengths and weaknesses.
- The results of the partner's previous joint ventures.
- The partner's ability to finance its portion of the deal, along with the capital market's view of the partner's investment. Not only is it important that the partner can make the investment, but also that *its* shareholders view the deal as a positive investment.
- The partner's competitive position, and why it is a better choice than its competitors.
- The objectives and prior investment history of any principals who finance the partner.

The Deal

Different deal structures suit different circumstances. Deals range from relatively straightforward arrangements—such as marketing and distribution agreements and technology licenses—to complex equity investments and joint ventures. For instance, some contingent equity investments, like earn-out structures, allow for partial investment at the beginning of the venture with increased investment over time based on achievement of various financial metrics.

This deal form is attractive in highly uncertain environments where the risk of not achieving projections is high. Others, like convertible structures, usually involve an exchange of value for a debt instrument with the option to convert the debt to equity. This gives some level of increased protection but has a higher up-front cost than an earn-out structure.

Effective boards discuss the appropriateness of the chosen deal structure with management and how it addresses key issues:

- *Risk preferences*: Which partner will fund any near-term investments (losses) and what incentives will it receive for this increased investment? To what extent does a partner require the cash flow investment to be convertible to an equity interest? What levels of exposure/risk are the partners willing to accept?
- *Liquidity*: How will the venture obtain additional financing? What is the exit strategy—how can we get out the joint venture if we want to? How can we take a bigger stake in the venture if it suits us? Can we have the new venture publicly registered, which would allow its equity to be traded?
- *Control*: How do windup provisions affect partners' control of the venture? If the business plan is not successfully executed, who has liquidation preference? Is our voting percentage fair in relation to our equity percentage?
- *Costs*: Are costs to be borne entirely by one party minimized, so both parties have incentive to control expenses? Is the portion of projected cost allocated to our company sustainable without an adverse impact on current operations?
- *Structure*: Should the new entity be set up as a general or limited liability partnership? As a taxable corporation?

Layered on these issues are the secondary effects of the joint venture on financial results. Management should be able to explain to the board whether the venture will dilute earnings, and the magnitude of change to financial ratios used to value the company. The board also needs confidence management has considered not only initial tax consequences, but also taxes during the venture operations and eventual windup.

The Homework

Due diligence is as important for these transactions as it is for mergers and acquisitions. Proper due diligence goes beyond a careful review of the transaction agreements. Board members want to be satisfied management has:

- Ensured that the quality of earnings/cash flow of the assets being contributed by the other partner has been audited.
- Identified and resolved business risks associated with the contributed assets. As a number of companies later learned, the strategic value of an asset is not necessarily reflected in financial

statements. One company, for example, invested an asset that was not directly generating positive income, only to realize later that the asset was a key part of its distribution network for other products.

- Carefully estimated the time to obsolescence of products constituting a critical portion of the value another partner is contributing.
- Separately identified and valued products our company is contributing, to ensure we don't include a highly profitable product without the proper compensation.

Major Capital Expenditures

Although not transformational in nature, major capital expenditures are certainly within the board's purview. The decision to build a major plant or acquire a new processing line could result in significant commitments of company assets. Management needs a disciplined process for identifying and analyzing capital projects. To avoid capital project failures, some companies have developed rigorous internal processes for vetting capital expenditure requests and following up on actual expenditures. It's common to find a formal management committee reviewing major expenditures. One company, stung by past problems, established such a committee comprising strategy, planning, environmental and technology people in addition to business unit representation. It independently assesses major projects before they go onward for formal board approval.

Board involvement ranges from approving specific capital projects exceeding a threshold, to approving the capital budget as a whole. Many directors like to see the entirety of the budget, believing it helps them understand the business. One director noted, "The best opportunity for meaningful input into a complex company is by approving the capital budget, because it gives directors an understanding of where resources are being used." Approving individual capital projects requires not only agreement on the threshold, but also keeping track of past project authorizations—experienced directors know to be on the lookout for a series of proposals each falling just below the threshold.

One director emphasizes the importance of bringing proposals to the board early, giving board members enough opportunity, over time, to absorb and become comfortable with a capital project. Another director seconded this concept, noting that if the board has input at an early stage in the process, outcomes are better than if directors first hear about a proposal when a formal expenditure request hits the board table.

While up-front board approval is common, reality is that boards often don't receive follow-up information covering the extent to which actual spending reflects the approved budget or whether an approved project was successful. For that reason, one director values post-expenditure audits of capital projects. She believes these allow both the board and management to get a real understanding of the capital project's outcome and value created. Moreover, post-expenditure audits alert management that the board is looking at the results of their decisions.

Experienced directors also look closely at projects, both in the authorization process and post authorization, for possible change in direction—whether strategic or tactical. One director insists her board be explicitly advised of any shift in program direction or scope, even though planned expenditures may be well within authorized limits.

CHAPTER 6
MANAGEMENT EVALUATION, COMPENSATION, AND SUCCESSION PLANNING

Board evaluation of senior management is critical to success of the company and its key executives. Objective, focused and constructive feedback helps executives develop their skills and abilities, and promotes success in steering the company toward its vision. And a sound evaluation process provides a clear basis for assignment and reward decisions.

While recognizing the need to evaluate the chief executive, even experienced directors often feel uneasy evaluating someone they perceive as being at least their peer. To handle this delicate task, highly effective boards establish clear-cut and comprehensive performance criteria and related metrics, as well as qualitative measures, for evaluating performance.

An Ongoing, Constructive Process for Evaluating the Chief Executive

Effective boards install a process combining development plans, ongoing monitoring and periodic formal assessments.

The process starts with the CEO's personal development plan, reflecting performance targets linked directly with corporate strategy and encompassing both short- and long-term company and personal goals. The board, or more commonly its evaluation/compensation committee, reviews the degree of success in achieving prior year's goals, as well as plans for the coming year, including strategic and business plans, budget forecasts and related goal setting. Properly done, this process obliges the CEO to maintain a long-term vision for the company, while still keeping an eye on short-term performance and rewards. Tools such as balanced scorecards allow nonfinancial metrics to be captured and tracked, so that other important objectives, like product innovation or retaining skilled performers, are identified in the plan as well.

It's critical the plans provide for development of any missing competencies needed for future success. Electronic commerce and knowledge management are transforming business. Related enabling competencies—strategy design, innovation, speed, risk taking and decisiveness—are not on everyone's radar screen today, yet are essential to future success.

Assessing executive performance must not be a once-a-year event. Performance needs continual monitoring, with results reviewed more fully at interim points during the year. Although interim assessments are less formal than an annual review, they're critical in allowing the board to act before minor problems become major.

Feedback typically is provided by the board chair, where the roles are separate. Otherwise it's done by a lead director, by the evaluation/compensation committee chair, or by an independent director to whom the board looks for leadership.

We know the best boards interact collegially with the chief executive, forming an effective working partnership. Does the evaluation process get in the way of that? It can, and how it's done and personalities involved can make or break this partnership. Experienced directors find using the right terminology can make a real difference in CEO receptivity to feedback. CEOs are not used to being "evaluated" and can bristle at the thought, but may be receptive to a "review" or "feedback" or "coaching" by respected board members.

Directors asking questions and discussing issues at board meetings are really providing feedback on management's proposals or ideas, and here, too, experienced directors find the method is as important as the content. A CEO of one company began pulling back, feeling the board was "throwing hand grenades" at him. The directors recognized and acknowledged a negative tone in their wording, and became more constructive in communications. It made a world of difference. Another CEO said the board was undermining him with frequent surprises in board meetings, bringing up issues "out of left field." After discussion the board agreed that just as it wouldn't want the CEO springing new issues at board meetings, this had to be a two-way street. Going forward the board apprised the CEO in advance about new issues, and the relationship immediately became more positive.

When receiving feedback, it's critical the CEO recognizes what is input or guidance, and what is directive. The board cannot expect the CEO to make this distinction if directors don't clearly differentiate. Directive comments will be infrequent, but when the board intends them as such, clarity is needed—if not in the formal meeting, then off-line.

Assessing the Intangibles — Beyond Performance Targets

In evaluating management the board should review not only whether targets have been met but also whether management, in hitting those targets, has properly positioned the company for future success. The board must consider the CEO's performance in developing leadership throughout the company. This directly affects the board's ability to deal with CEO succession and to ensure senior management, overall, is highly competent, motivated and functioning effectively as a well-balanced team.

Most boards recognize how critically important it is for senior management to set the right "tone at the top." But board focus on this key issue is often lacking. Effective boards encourage senior management to define, refine and demonstrate company values that include essential cultural factors such as honesty, dedication, flexibility, openness, innovation, teamwork and respect. They look at the extent to which management leads by example and has created a culture that will perpetuate the characteristics that make the company successful and resilient.

In addition to values leadership, some boards specifically evaluate other factors, for example, decision making. The CEO performs a self-assessment, rating elements such as the extent of decisiveness, inclusion of others in decisions, seeking input from others, explaining decisions and making realistic decisions. Direct reports rate the CEO on those issues in a 360-degree process, and the board rates the CEO as well. Each of these ratings is presented to the CEO on a confidential basis. By repeating the process annually, the CEO can see how others perceive him or her over time and assess progress. One should not expect this process to be immediately trusted by either the senior manager raters or the CEO. But if it is done with consistency and integrity, trust is earned, and the results can be extremely beneficial.

Once the full evaluation is complete, results are confidentially communicated to the CEO, along with recommendations to be incorporated into his/her development plan. Some boards find it helpful to use a professional "coach" in developing the evaluation and analyzing and communicating the results. For feedback to other executives, the board typically provides review results to the CEO, who discusses them with the respective senior managers.

Incentives and Rewards

Which brings us to another tough issue—how to incent and reward the chief executive to best achieve both short- and long-term corporate goals, and to attract and retain the best talent. How well a board handles the often immense pressure coming from forceful and highly charged executives, who may be in great demand by competitors and other companies, can make the difference between long-term effective leadership and a harmful series of changes at the top. The intense scrutiny of compensation packages by investors and analysts only complicates this further.

Key to effectively dealing with compensation is ensuring that directors doing the evaluating and compensation setting are truly independent. While there are many definitions of independence, the critical element is a spirit of independence. Simply stated, directors must not be beholden to management in any way. Boards typically form an evaluation and compensation committee, insulating independent directors' discussion.

Determining the right compensation package in an environment of economic and market volatility provides particular challenges. In a business environment where public perception, enhanced by media attention, doesn't always view management compensation as fair, boards need to navigate based on a clear and well-understood compensation philosophy grounded in performance. Progressive boards no longer focus solely on internally generated performance targets, but look also to external benchmarks from peer companies or industry performance indexes in setting performance standards.

Effective boards make sure compensation packages for the CEO and senior management directly align with the company's business strategy and value drivers. For example, e-commerce and other "new economy" businesses commonly pay relatively low cash compensation but provide a sizeable equity stake. But this type of package must be kept current. The result in one particular company is not atypical, where once the company's proven success was established, the compensation package wasn't realigned with new initiatives and goals. The net effect was that the CEO was incented not to drive share value, but rather to arrange to sell the company.

What do effective boards do in shaping compensation? Experience of major companies offers insight into best practice.

- Fundamental is granting options and performance shares, as well as establishing share ownership guidelines for senior executives. In this way boards align interests of individuals with those of shareholders. If it is done well, executives and particularly the CEO are incented to make hard choices for the long-term health and prosperity of the business. But some practices can be counterproductive, such as continually repricing options so executives stay "in the money." While repricing may be appropriate in some circumstances—like when options become a disincentive and start to drive people away, or when the company performs comparatively well during an industry-wide downturn—it can defeat the underlying purpose of the incentive if done without good cause.
- Boards are expanding pay opportunities for CEOs but tying increases to substantial performance achievement. By designing upward leverage into CEO pay packages for delivering performance results, boards can be more demanding of CEOs to achieve performance gains.
- With heavy emphasis on linking senior executive and shareholder interests through stock ownership, boards seek to ensure management is focused not solely on short-term stock price increases, but on a range of strategic and operating goals. Stock price gains need to be over the long term. Progressive boards have adopted balanced scorecards designed to fit the business' value drivers, measuring results against forward-looking indicators of business health such as new customers, distribution channels and product introductions.
- Forward-thinking boards recognize that value creators in today's complex business enterprises extend well beyond the CEO to other key executives. These boards have narrowed the gap between long-term-based compensation packages for the CEO and other senior executives. Results include building better teamwork in the executive group and enhancing overall performance. Perhaps surprising to some, executives of some companies

recognize this issue, evidenced by the CEO of one company who advised the board considering special compensation not to grant it, wanting not to "ruin the team feeling we have going in my management group."

One of the most difficult challenges for boards is determining "how much is enough" to motivate the CEO and management team. In these days of mega stock option grants and jumbo golden parachutes, boards must weigh demands of the competitive market with their fiduciary responsibility to shareholders. Although boards often rely on a competitive analysis of CEOs in similar companies, more boards now look at compensation growth in relation to increase in shareholder wealth creation. Tying CEO and senior management compensation to factors described above, as well as measures such as increase in market capitalization, return on equity and cash flow, can motivate effort and focus and link them with long-term growth.

A corporate governance thought leader bemoaned the ballooning size of American CEO compensation packages: "It seems as though no board ever wants to say that they are paying their CEOs less than the top quartile. Even the boards of the poorest performing companies believe they need to pay in the top quartile to either attract or retain the talent that they hope will lead them out of the problems." While attracting the right talent takes money or wealth-creation potential or both, boards inadvertently can send the message that they will pay for underperformance. Many directors expressed similar concerns about the unhealthy ratcheting up of compensation.

But there are cases of insufficient pay packages. The CEO of a large retail company demanded "mega" options, claiming that with superior stock price performance, option grants had not kept pace with shareholder gains as a percentage of market capitalization. With analysis, the board agreed and appropriately granted additional options.

Effective compensation and incentive programs require knowledge of the marketplace, competitive forces and the enterprise's value drivers, and recognition of the benefits of retaining an effective chief executive. A strong "fact base" of data can be generated through industry reports, published survey information, analysis of proxy information and custom surveys. Boards look to the company's own human resources function and sometimes consultants for information and analysis in designing the right package.

A Call to Action – Replacing the Chief Executive

Perhaps the most difficult action a board takes is replacing a chief executive. When is it necessary? What prompts the decision? How does the board know?

In many cases where the board made a change, action was prompted by the company not "making the numbers." In others a strategic blunder, or a fraud or personal indiscretion, forced the board to act. In one well-publicized case it wasn't just missing the expected results, but a case of the chief executive and his CFO being "less than forthcoming" in answering direct questions from the board.

But in most cases a need to make a change at the top is far from clear-cut, and most directors want nothing less than to have to deal with such a drastic move. They recognize the corporate and personal pain associated with removing the chief executive. However, boards are demonstrating an increasing willingness to make the tough calls. Indeed, many directors interviewed have removed the CEOs from their companies.

What's the answer? At the risk of being overly simplistic, the better boards have set clear expectations, put measurement processes in place and provide ongoing monitoring and feedback—that is, they're doing the things outlined above with substance and effect. Headlines are rife with companies thrown into crisis where a board seemingly decided abruptly to remove the CEO. But in many of those cases in fact there was no crisis—the board had done its job well and was well prepared, and the company well positioned, for transition to a new leader.

Nonetheless, too many boards have been blindsided. They didn't have critical insight into problems that had long been brewing, and then acted precipitously or much too late. Yes, there are circumstances when something comes out of the blue, but most frequently if the board had been doing all along what it should have been doing, there would be no crisis.

There's another real issue with which boards must come to grips—dealing with a forceful and powerful chief executive. We've seen companies with such a leader whose performance was no longer cutting it, where the board didn't have the courage to take on the CEO. In addition to having the evaluative processes in place and functioning effectively, the board must have the mechanisms and wherewithal to take action when required, no matter how difficult. The mechanisms cannot be put in place when major problems surface. The board needs to look well in advance at its ability when under stress to take the requisite action.

Apart from a forceful CEO, directors also may find themselves dealing with the company founder, whose vision and drive built the company and whose personality has become the company brand. The sense of loyalty directors may feel to such a CEO—who likely recruited them to the board in the first place and made the company a past success—makes it especially difficult to identify when that founder ceases to be effective. The board at one such successful company let an ineffective founder remain far beyond his productive life—running shareholder value down in the process. In such a situation, once again, a clear planning and evaluation process can help identify whether a founder lacks the competencies and skills to take the company to the next stage. Although the removal of a charismatic company founder is never easy, a defined process may remove some of the pain.

Assessing Senior Managers

Directors' attention is aimed primarily at the CEO, as the company leader reporting directly to the board. But effective boards also look closely at other members of the senior management team. This helps ensure the CEO is supplementing his or her own strengths with a team capable in areas where the CEO is not as strong. This is best done by assessing the CEO's process for evaluating his/her direct reports and other executives critical to the company's success. The board looks at how executives' performance is assessed against expectations. The process should relate performance to specific agreed-upon criteria that consider how well executives achieved financial and nonfinancial objectives, progress made and contributions to implementing corporate strategy.

Experience shows that many boards don't give sufficient attention to evaluation of senior executives below the CEO. Inadequate attention is compounded where a CEO is reluctant to pass critical judgment on colleagues he/she mentored, helped promote or has long-term personal ties with. By ensuring an objective and rigorous evaluation of senior management, the board can help get past these natural inhibitors, ensuring development and retention of the caliber of talent essential to support company success. Top performers as well as underachievers must be identified, and rewards, remedial steps or removal initiated as necessary.

An effective technique a number of boards use is to see that the CEO has senior managers self-assess their performance against specified targets. The board, or more commonly a committee, reviews the CEO's analysis, forming an independent judgment. In addition to evaluating against targets, progress is reviewed against prior developmental recommendations.

Succession Planning and CEO Selection

In theory, if a company has done an outstanding job of attracting, motivating, developing and retaining the best human resources, management succession and identification of the next chief executive will evolve naturally. The board would seldom need to look outside for the next leader. But of course we don't live in a theoretical world. A recent study shows two-thirds of boards have no defined process to look at CEO succession.

Regardless of the current CEO's strength, at some point a successor will be needed. The board must face the reality that that might occur well in advance of when currently anticipated. Effective boards make sure bench strength is there, so that any of several executives are ready, or are on track to soon be ready, to step up to the top job.

How best to ensure this? One effective approach is to make this one of the current CEO's responsibilities, with board oversight. The CEO is charged with responsibility to groom a senior management team having a pool of potential successors. Certainly not every senior executive needs to fall into that category. But the CEO needs to make sure attention is given to this critical issue.

How does a board select a new corporate leader? A disciplined process streamlines the task and makes it effective. A first step is to define selection criteria. The board will consider the attributes, competencies and values identified as necessary to successfully lead the company—things like vision, strategic thinking, decision making, knowledge, communications, energy, experience, intelligence, leadership, ethics and values, team building. Other factors noted as important include being passionate and consistent, philosophical yet action oriented and hands-on, and being close to employees and customers. Being close to customers, to take the last example, enables an executive to learn about the customer's vision and how it plans to get there, providing crucial information about innovations the company needs to link with the customer's vision.

Advisors on this issue emphasize one overriding point—that the most effective boards focus mainly on what the company needs to succeed not in its current business, but rather in the businesses of the future.

Identifying prospective candidates among current company executives should be relatively straightforward. This is the case when directors have been focusing all along on the senior management team's performance. Regular exposure to senior managers provides an important perspective that can be crucial when looking for the next leader.

Identifying qualified external candidates can take more effort. Directors often have extensive personal networks of business leaders, and the best boards take full advantage of this knowledge and access. Regardless, most boards enlist the services of executive search firms to identify a larger pool of qualified candidates. The board committee typically empowered to conduct the search needs to be certain the search firm fully understands the fabric of and vision for the company, as well as its specific selection criteria. If certain criteria are more important than others, the weighting should be communicated as well.

The more thoughtful and comprehensive the process, the higher the likelihood a number of highly qualified candidates will emerge. Best board practice involves a series of meetings, formal and informal, with candidates and directors, individually or in groups of directors or the entire board. Sometimes called "getting to know you" sessions, these are where each director forms a judgment on which candidate has the qualities warranting a decision to entrust him or her with the future of the company.

At this point there's no formula. Directors have said it comes down to gut feel. This doesn't mean a quick or haphazard approach. Rather, with several outstanding candidates, directors bring their knowledge, experience and seasoned judgment to bear in making this most important decision.

A Broader Look at Human Capital

This chapter is primarily about the CEO and senior management. But the best boards devote as much attention to whether and how the company makes sure it has the people throughout the organization necessary to achieve the company's goals. To paraphrase one observer, who used a now common phrase for emphasis, "It's not the strategy—it's the implementation, stupid!" He adds, "Companies with outstanding strategies have failed for not having the right people to carry it out, or lacking the creativity and ability to change to keep the company vibrant. Conversely, companies with mediocre strategy, comprised of people having those qualities, have been wildly successful."

Effective boards make sure the senior management team has the processes in place, and the requisite culture, to attract, recruit, develop, reward and retain the right people. We've long heard about movement from an agricultural to an industrial to a knowledge-based society. Knowledge, and how to use it effectively, is about people, and there's nothing more important than having the right people with a shared vision and passionate about achieving it. And beyond that there needs to be alignment of the people, process and incentives with corporate strategy.

While one size does not fit all companies, successful enterprises seem to attract and retain people who are passionate and excited about the business. The board needs to look closely at whether the chief executive and senior management team have set that kind of environment, and underlying business processes are in place to make it work. This is not just about human resources systems, although they're important. It's about mission, vision, culture, environment, management style, process, openness, respect, values, and more. For a company to have success over the long haul, it must get this right, and the board needs to make sure it does.

CHAPTER 7
TELLING THE WORLD

With increased competition for capital, globalization has led to calls for consistent financial reporting standards, increased "transparency" and greater disclosure. Investors and analysts base decisions on the information they receive—much of it coming directly from companies themselves. The less they trust that information, the less they're willing to pay for the company's securities, and the higher the company's cost of capital.

Companies found misreporting information face great risk and severe consequences. Examples abound. In an investor conference call, the CEO hid the nature of an improvement in company performance. Later, when it was learned that a one-time extraordinary gain was reported as operating revenue—with reporting practices changed to disguise the unusual item—the markets reacted, driving the stock price down to a 52-week low. Similar punishment has been meted out to other companies discovered playing games.

Traditional Financial Reporting and Related Regulatory Disclosures

Because of their impact on the cost of capital and share price, communications to the capital markets are of critical importance. Financial results have long been the cornerstone of these communications, with annual and interim financial statements the key report cards. As such, board involvement with these disclosures is vital.

Boards in many countries delegate responsibility for overseeing financial reporting to their audit committees. In many parts of the world, publicly listed companies are required to have such committees, while elsewhere they may be recommended. Best practices for audit committees are becoming well established, and include steps an audit committee, or full board, should take when approving key financial communications. These are summarized in Exhibit 7.1. Only some of the key points of focus are highlighted here, with a fuller discussion contained in the companion document to this report, titled *Audit Committee Effectiveness — What Works Best, 2nd Edition.* That report provides advice to audit committee members and other directors interested in this topic.

Directors recognize the importance of annual earnings reports, and the process surrounding release of annual earnings is typically rigorous—usually more so than that around interim reports. But pressure for earnings management can be just as intense with regard to interim results, and sometimes more difficult to resist. Experienced directors recognize these pressures and give requisite attention to all public financial reports.

These pressures have been in the sights of securities regulators, who now have little tolerance for "earnings management," pointing to its ability to erode confidence in the capital markets. Although the practice of "borrowing" earnings from future periods is guaranteed to fail in the long term, some companies still try it. Recently regulators have looked more closely at practices like storing earnings for a rainy day, which companies claim is acceptable under the banner of "conservative accounting." At its extreme, earnings management is followed by restatement of previously reported earnings, removal of senior executives and pummeled stock price.

Directors at some companies have, unfortunately, been too trusting, and they need to take off their blinders to the threat of earnings manipulation. The best boards carefully review and discuss areas most subject to manipulation. They have members with past experience in financial reporting, who can and do ask insightful questions, delving into the fairness of to-be-reported results. These boards also compare results against benchmarks and other performance measures, and the broader economic picture, to see whether, in those contexts, the results make sense.

There can be harsh consequences from inadequate disclosure of other required regulatory information. One securities regulator found that a company's proxy statement didn't fully disclose substantial financial benefits provided to the retiring CEO or a significant related party transaction with the CEO's son. Directors knew about the transactions, but nonetheless approved the regulatory filings. By the time the regulator finalized its action, many of those directors had been removed from the board, which shrank in size from 24 members to nine.

In addition to financial statements, public companies may be required to disclose other information such as:

- *Executive compensation and remuneration*, covering responsibilities for and approach to overseeing executive compensation, typical elements of remuneration (salary, bonuses, stock options, etc.) and the level of compensation for key executives.
- *Corporate governance activities*, describing corporate governance systems and level of compliance with recommended governance guidelines.

Boards should be satisfied the information they're required to approve fits with their understanding, and take any additional steps needed to feel comfortable with the reliability of the information and underlying processes.

Exhibit 7.1: The Board's Involvement in Financial Reporting

Item	Board's Typical Duties
Annual and Interim Financial Reports:	• Understand process management has instituted to ensure relevant financial transactions are captured and reported • Review major accounting policies and concur on their appropriateness; understand reasons for any policy changes • Understand major weaknesses in internal control over financial reporting, and impact on financial systems and reports • Discuss control weaknesses and other relevant issues with internal audit • Review and discuss the financial statements with management • Determine nature of any major disagreements between management and external auditor • Discuss financial statements, auditor's report, any qualifications and nature of adjustments required with external auditor • Approve financial statements once satisfied they are appropriate
Narrative Reporting (sometimes called Management Discussion or Operating Review)	• Review and understand disclosures proposed • Inquire whether disclosure complies with regulatory requirements • Determine its consistency and completeness, based on board's understanding of what has happened in the business • Discuss whether report format and quality support company's reputation • Approve as appropriate

Disclosing Operating Information

While traditional financial disclosures are important, markets utilize a lot of other information as well, and the nature of information deemed relevant evolves quickly. Internet companies, for example, rack up huge market capitalization without ever having turned a profit, as analysts and investors focus on data such as number of subscribers, time on-line and peak volumes. When one such company released numbers on the level of new subscribers midquarter, its share price jumped by more than it had ever moved on earnings releases.

Not all board members fully recognize the risks associated with assembling and communicating nonfinancial information. Reality is that this information:

- Typically originates in areas of the company where personnel aren't always familiar with the critical importance of information reliability.
- Often isn't subject to the same review processes that finance departments have in place to check reliability of financial information.
- Might not be reported consistently from one period to the next.
- Isn't bound by standard definitions—either in the industry or even within the company. Thus, for example, comparing the number of "access lines" reported by different telecommunications companies might be akin to comparing apples and oranges.
- Usually is not subject to audit.

Reporting wrong nonfinancial information has left companies with egg on their face. In a widely publicized case, an automobile manufacturer overstated one month's unit sales, based on inflated numbers provided by dealers. The overstatement didn't result in reporting incorrect financial results, but the data was to be used in marketing campaigns. The company uncovered its own mistake, and its credibility wasn't terribly damaged, but it suffered some degree of embarrassment when it publicly admitted the error and issued revised numbers.

Effective boards recognize the relevance of operating information management releases and monitor these measures regularly. Indeed, these boards question management on information accuracy, probing what controls are in place and what verifications are made of this publicly reported information.

Disclosure Practices

The board's understanding of what information is released and how management ensures its reliability, is important, but that's just the starting point. How and when the company discloses information to analysts, shareholders and others is also crucial.

One company learned its lesson the hard way. It was accused of disclosing weaker than expected sales to one analyst one week before making the information available publicly. The analyst relayed the news to his clients, who sold the stock before the price fell. Class action lawsuits ensued and the securities regulator launched an investigation. Regulators are looking more broadly at "selective disclosure," with the U.S. Securities and Exchange Commission formulating rules to crack down on the practice.

Knowledgeable boards look at and behind their companies' communications policies and processes. They proactively see to it that the likelihood of problems in communicating sensitive information—potentially damaging reputation or inviting regulatory action—is minimal. These boards want to see clear, effective processes encompassing best practices such as:

- A clearly designated and skilled spokesperson to handle external communications.
- Explicit policies instructing others that they are not authorized to speak on behalf of the company.
- Updated policies addressing new technologies, including forbidding employees from sharing company information in Internet chat rooms or posting it on message boards.
- Mechanisms to monitor messages and compliance with policies, enabling any inadvertent slips—or flagrant violations—to be dealt with by timely, corrective disclosure, and disciplinary action if warranted.
- "Quiet" periods in advance of earnings announcements, when the company doesn't comment on earnings.
- Issuing a news release *before* discussing results with analysts or others.
- Communications policies covering board members themselves, so that all company communications move through designated channels.

With current technological capabilities, companies have little excuse for not leveling the communications playing field. Steps can be taken to ensure that all interested parties have access to the same information at the same time. Companies now open up quarterly conference calls with analysts to individual investors and the media. Some use the Internet to broadcast meetings or conference calls. Others post relevant information on their website in investor relations areas.

Are there challenges in using new technology? You bet. Companies fall down when they don't update their websites timely with information just announced in news releases. Conversely, companies could inadvertently post information on their website before approved for formal release. And, in the same way the internet makes it easy for companies to communicate their messages widely at little cost, it also allows individuals to air their concerns.

How can boards contribute in addressing these challenges? By:

- Impressing on management the unacceptability of treating various stakeholders and the market inequitably.
- Reviewing communications policies and provisions for authorizing selected individuals to speak for the company.
- Considering how new technologies are being used or contemplated.
- Evaluating practices management has implemented to vet the communication of important information.
- Reviewing remedial actions for any material information that was released inappropriately.

Experienced directors take care that they themselves don't become part of the disclosure problem. They avoid putting themselves on the firing line with the press and potentially letting critical information slip out. And they've learned the danger of talking in crowded elevators or restaurants, and remember that fellow passengers can overhear airplane conversations.

Market Sensitive Developments

In the age of the merger, what information gets disclosed, to whom and when are crucial considerations. Getting the timing and nature of these disclosures wrong can derail a deal, harm investor value and bring scrutiny by regulators. Traditionally, companies disclose a deal when they've reached agreement on price and structure, but specific requirements vary by country. Legal counsel can guide the company through the timing and nature of specific disclosures that apply when deals are in the offing. How do skilled directors avoid difficulties? They make sure:

- The company has in place a policy spelling out on what matters it will and won't comment, and that those who speak for the company are trained in its application. Such a policy provides a simple but effective safety device—it allows company spokespersons when questioned to say truthfully: "It's company policy not to comment on potential acquisitions."
- The policy sets out expectations for employees who know about the merger/transaction discussions—those who have been "brought over the wall."
- Management has a process for informing such individuals of the policy.
- Management has procedures to track who knew what, and when they knew it, with a clear-cut list of individuals who are "over the wall." The company's ability to track this information is, in a number of countries, central to protecting itself and its employees against charges of insider trading.
- The board reviews reports on insider trading. These may involve an overview of the trading approval process and a conclusion from the general counsel of overall policy compliance and whether insiders abstained from trading during restricted windows.

Directors also need to realize that they themselves are insiders on the transaction, and ensure they don't get offside on the confidentiality or trading rules.

Communications in Times of Crisis

When a crisis hits, a company has many choices to make, including what to communicate to outside parties and when. More than a decade after the fact, Johnson & Johnson still receives kudos for its handling of the Tylenol product tampering, including effective and timely public communications.

Other crises, such as the sudden death of a key executive or discovery of accounting irregularities, need to be addressed appropriately. Experience shows the great importance of an explicit protocol having been established in advance, so that when a bomb drops the key players know exactly what to do. Response plans need to encompass a communications component—ensuring the right information is provided to the board and the right message released to the public. Typically during a crisis board members are in close contact with senior management, agreeing on communications and using the predetermined channels to disseminate information.

Disclosing the Board's Own Practices

Disclosures about the board itself and its committees can assure shareholders that practices are in place to promote both director and management accountability. In some countries, regulators or stock exchanges require specific disclosures. Whether or not mandated, the board may wish to provide relevant governance information. Exhibit 7.2 shows elements of board operations that might be disclosed. Some companies, like General Motors, have chosen to publish their boards' governance guidelines.

Exhibit 7.2: Board Disclosures on Governance

- Board mandate, responsibilities and roles
- Board composition, size, proportion of independent directors, etc.
- Existence, membership and mandates of board committees
- Proportion of independent directors
- Existence of board assessment process
- Selection and orientation of new directors
- Director compensation
- Extent of directors' shareholdings in the company
- Numbers of board and committee meetings and attendance rates

Particular concerns around financial reporting have resulted in increased, mandatory disclosure about audit committees and their activities. For instance, the SEC now requires that registered companies disclose information on:

- *Audit committee independence*, covering the independence of committee members and discussing reasons for appointing any nonindependent director to the committee
- *Audit committee charter*, with publication of the charter at least every three years
- *Audit committee activities*, including the committee's review and discussion of the audited financial statements with management, and discussion with the auditors on significant matters and auditor independence

The Bottom Line

Communications and disclosure are more complex, not less, despite the advances of technology. Technology allows companies to disseminate information easily, but also allows disgruntled employees to broadcast unauthorized views. Successful directors play their part in ensuring their companies communicate reliable, relevant and timely information—whether favorable or unfavorable—to those who need it.

CHAPTER 8
BOARD DYNAMICS

The days of rubber stamping management's decisions, collecting fees and adjourning for lunch are over—at least for most boards. Some are models of effective governance, doing the job as intended. Unlike the failures, which attract widespread attention, good boards function quietly and efficiently, serving shareholder-constituents in pursuit of growing long-term shareholder value.

Why are some boards highly effective at carrying out the responsibilities outlined in previous chapters, and others not? Why are some stuck in the past?

It's difficult if not impossible to do the right thing if a board is dysfunctional. The best boards have adopted a culture and operating style enabling them and management to operate effectively together. Some boards have not. This chapter is about the good and the bad of board functionality. Few boards are at one extreme. Where does your board stand on this continuum of bad and good? No doubt you'll recognize characteristics falling at various points.

The Bad

Boards can be susceptible to a wide range of dysfunctional practices:

- The chief executive sees the board as a burden on management, its influence to be minimized. The board is a necessary evil, consisting of part-time observers and outsiders knowing little about the business and second-guessing management. It's simply another layer of bureaucracy getting in way of getting things done.
- Management keeps directors in dark, providing as little information as possible and avoiding threatening issues. A good meeting is short, routine and side steps important issues.
- The chief executive sets rigid agendas and runs tightly regimented, formal meetings. Directors are expected not to interrupt highly structured presentations.
- Board meetings don't provide a forum for raising and discussing serious issues. Management is impatient with directors not immediately sharing full commitment to the presented path. Regular board meetings are an unsuitable if not a hostile environment for revealing serious reservations about intended directions.
- Directors are beholden to the chief executive.

- Directors violating norms of boardroom debate by aggressively challenging corporate leadership run the risk of finding themselves isolated and possibly replaced.
- Virtually all information comes from management, making meaningful assessment of strategic direction and operating plans difficult at best.
- Lack of insightful analysis makes it difficult for the board to interpret and act timely on signs of impending trouble. Problems are buried in the numbers, without focus on relevant action options. A director who does see early warning signals is viewed as an alarmist or a "Chicken Little."

Ineffective boards often are failures of board culture. They operate on the basis of unwritten and unspoken rules. An established pecking order exists, not immediately obvious. Directors are passive, accepting, defer to the chair and support management no matter what. This culture can be tremendously resistant to change. For a new director wanting to make things better, inertia and resistance can be an incredible challenge.

The Good

What do effective boards do? Simply put, the opposite of the above. And changing a "bad" board culture to a "good" one is not easy. Focusing on the following should help.

Board Composition

A board's composition is fundamental to its effectiveness. Boards need to have a degree of independence from management, have the right people at the table and be of manageable size to function well.

Independence

A board that's beholden to management cannot be effective. This doesn't necessarily mean a board hand-picked by a CEO is doomed to failure. There are a number of cases where such boards have done a great job, and even stood up to and dismissed the CEO when necessary. But the board cannot at the same time both be subservient to the chief executive and insist on doing what needs to be done.

In many countries there's no issue, because the board chair and chief executive jobs are separate. That's the case, for example, in the United Kingdom for reportedly more than 70 percent of large public companies. By contrast, in the United States the figure is reportedly less than 20 percent.

Boards that combine the role of chair and chief executive can take any of a number of actions to ensure effective functioning in the face of a strong chair/chief executive:

- *Independent majority* – Maintaining a majority of directors with no ties to the company or its leader can serve as a healthy counterbalance to the CEO/chair. Similar independence of key committee memberships further promotes effective oversight.
- *Robust nominating committee* – Selection of new members is critical to bringing the right talent to the board, and a nominating committee comprising strong, independent directors can make all the difference.
- *Strong corporate governance committee* – This committee of independent directors can provide leadership to the board on critical governance activities.
- *Lead director* – One independent director is designated as the conduit bringing ideas, feedback and direction to the CEO/chair. In some instances the lead director focuses on board effectiveness, letting the chief executive concentrate primarily on running the company, and also chairs board sessions held without management present.

These are not mutually exclusive, with some boards employing all these measures. But generally the first three are most widely accepted, while the fourth is not. Some favor a lead director, believing it acts as a good counterbalance and avoids fragmented or mixed messages. But most boards and observers don't support the concept, on the basis it can inappropriately dilute the CEO's power, create rivalry leading to compromise rather than decisiveness, and result in two public spokespersons and related confusion.

The objectives of a lead director can be achieved in a way that's more widely embraced. Frequently one independent director emerges naturally who is looked to as a nonexecutive leader. Omitting the formal designation seems to avoid the negativity.

Another tactic effective boards find useful is to hold "executive" sessions of only outside directors. Typically held after each board meeting, directors freely discuss issues and concerns without management present. It provides an opportunity to assess what went well in the meeting and what they would like to see in future meetings, with one director selected to provide feedback to the CEO.

Seasoned CEOs recognize the benefits of such executive sessions, for both the board and management. In one case, though, the chief executive routinely dropped in on meetings to observe the proceedings. Off-line discussion with the CEO on the reason for meetings without management present clarified the protocol.

An experienced board member advises, "It is essential to set up a practice of having independent directors meeting regularly—and don't wait for a crisis—do it when things are calm."

What it comes down to is the willingness of independent directors to challenge the CEO when necessary. One seasoned director sees a clear trend in this direction, with boards increasingly "suggesting alterations to CEO proposals or, in the extreme, going through the effort to remove a CEO. General Motors was a landmark case, and independent directors have since found a voice and are using it."

Characteristics

We all know the characteristics directors should have. One list identifies integrity, accountability, credibility, trustworthiness, strategic thinking, intuition, vision, expertise in where the company is going, knowledge of the future of the industry, communication skills, effective decision-making style, good interpersonal and interactive skills, and ability to handle conflict. Others include active participation, willingness to listen, analytical skills, and judgment.

Much can be and has been written on this. What it comes down to is having the right skill sets and strength of character to do the right thing for the company and its shareholders, even if it's not always popular.

Size

Yes, board size truly is critical.

For years many boards were too large. Large boards can potentially limit directors' participation in discussing key issues, allow a manipulative CEO to control the board by divide-and-rule tactics and reduce flexibility to call meetings on short notice in response to crises without key members being absent.

A long-time director recalls a bank board where "there were 30 to 35 people on the board, and I could hardly see the person at the other end. I think seven to nine board members are appropriate." Another director said, "Once you get beyond 10 or 12 people on a board, you don't discuss—you wait for your turn to speak. " This sentiment about very large boards is widely shared, and in recent years size has come down. Boards of perhaps seven to twelve members are more common.

But there have been some signs of reversal. Boards are looking for particular expertise in technology in general and e-business in particular, in new industries or markets and in global knowledge, and are adding members where needed.

Of course, one size does not fit all. The right size brings the requisite knowledge, abilities and skills to the table in a group small enough to act cohesively.

How a Board Functions

There are no rules for how board meetings should be conducted or how directors should act. But there are commonalties among highly effective boards. These boards:

- Have an atmosphere of openness and trust. Directors feel free to speak their minds, and pursue issues to their appropriate conclusion. There is also cohesiveness in objective and method.
- Establish roles that are understood and embraced. Directors bring fresh ideas and constructive tension and feedback. The CEO seeks out and values the board.
- Balance thought and thoroughness with speed and decisiveness. Sufficient thought and creativity are brought to decisions on strategy and major programs, and good chemistry and trust enable the company to seize fleeting opportunities where necessary.

The dynamics of board–management interaction is fertile ground for psychologists, and we're not going to delve deeply into this topic. But one issue on the minds of many directors involves the nature and timing of information the CEO shares with the board. Directors want to know "what's on the mind of the CEO," learning about important matters as they evolve. They want fewer reports after the fact, more about concerns before formal plans are formulated. They say the CEO is more credible by sharing troubling issues early on. Directors don't want major surprises and don't want always to be "sold" on predetermined plans. And as one observer said, "To me, a CEO who always has an immediate answer to every question is suspect. My sense is he is overly arrogant and not sharing real concerns."

But this can be a double-edged sword. Directors also don't want a CEO who doesn't have his/her arms around issues, or appears indecisive or even worse, weak. CEOs perceived as such have found themselves immersed dealing with "too much help" from the board. As with most things, striking the right balance is all-important.

Board Meetings

Many directors have indicated disappointment with how board meetings are conducted. They say meetings are too rigid, allow too little time for important issues and don't have the right atmosphere, and they are provided deficient advance material. They say there's too much reporting and too little discussion, or dialogue is cut off too quickly. The agenda has the wrong topics, or wrong sequence, and their fellow directors don't prepare sufficiently.

Many board chairs, with input and support of their fellow directors, structure and run effective board meetings. This is not rocket science. They avoid the "bad" practices identified above and embrace the "good" and the board works well. Much has been written on conducting effective meetings, which need not be repeated here.

Additional insight may be gained, however, by the experiences and suggestions of directors who have seen the good and the bad. Here's what they recommend:

- The CEO must believe that he/she can learn from the board. Implied but unstated is that the board must believe that's what the CEO believes.
- Watch the basics: Get advance buy-in on the agenda, get the right amount of good advance material out on a timely basis, put tough issues first, avoid bureaucracy, limit presentations to allow full dialogue and provide cushion allowing additional time if needed.
- The board should seek the "collective wisdom" of its members. In many instances that collective wisdom does not get out because the group is not a group. There's a lack of leadership, time and trust. Time should be taken to build relationships in social settings, as well as formal ones. This is crucial to getting the most out of boards.
- The board should seek out and discuss information other than that provided by management.
- Use good judgment in delivering criticism. Directors need to know when to deliver criticism at full board meetings and when to deliver it in private session with the CEO.
- With young, entrepreneurial CEOs and the warp speed pace of acquisitions, balance the need to ensure good decisions are made with the CEO's need to "strike while the iron is hot." This new breed of CEO may want to conduct board meetings on the phone at the drop of a hat, but live meetings normally are better because they allow important nonverbal reactions and ability to halt action where appropriate.
- Use board retreats to spend adequate time on strategy and other critical issues.
- Directors need to see their role as a process, not an event. That is, they need to feel continuous responsibility for overseeing their companies and not confine their efforts to merely attending board meetings.
- Don't spend much time looking at the past. Spend more time discussing forward strategic direction.

This advice suggests that while meeting effectiveness is important to board effectiveness, activity occurring outside the boardroom is as, or perhaps even more, critical.

Trust needs to develop among directors and with management, and is vital to group dynamics and a board's effectiveness. Relationships cannot develop solely in a boardroom. Many board leaders recognize this and provide for director interaction outside meetings. Frequent exchanges by phone among directors are seen as much more positive than divisive.

How many times have we seen a board member raise an issue, get no reaction and drop the matter quickly? Successful directors take the time to discuss issues before meetings and either get needed support before tabling the concern, or be reassured it's not important.

Another director reported being browbeaten by management until finally forced to resign. An effective board would not permit this. Trust and cohesiveness among directors means they will support one another when appropriate, regardless of the CEO's initial position, and won't ostracize a fellow director pursuing a controversial yet relevant issue. Issues and board members are dealt with fairly and openly in a positive, constructive environment.

Executive sessions, mentioned earlier, are normally supplemented by off-line discussions among independent directors. The venue varies, evidenced by directors of one company riding together to the airport after a board meeting. The CEO had pushed for employment contracts for all senior management candidates. Conversation on the topic was deferred until arrival at the airport, when out of earshot of the corporate driver, and the group quickly made a decision that contracts were undesirable, with one director given responsibility to get back to the CEO.

Charter

Best practice calls for a written charter, outlining responsibilities, structure, membership criteria and process.

Specific board requirements may be set forth in national or local legislation, stock exchange listing requirements, court rulings and corporate bylaws. Charters should reflect these rules, or at least be consistent with them. The company's legal counsel typically is intimately involved in ensuring legal and other requirements are met in developing and updating the charter.

A board charter provides a foundation and focal point for board activities. But to be useful, it needs to be referenced periodically to measure conformance. Even more important, directors should recognize that no charter can foresee the future and capture all activities a board will face over time. So while the charter is useful and should be a periodic reference point, it should not serve as the day-to-day driver of activity, or as a limiting factor in doing what needs to be done to best serve the company's and shareholder interests.

Charters typically address the topics outlined in Exhibit 8.1.

Exhibit 8.1: Board Charters

Board Responsibilities	Discussion of major responsibilities, including which are carried out by a board committee; distinction of board responsibilities from management responsibilities
Board Composition	Size of board; proportion of independent directors to management directors; definition of independence applied; term limits; retirement age; limits on number of directorships
Director Selection	Selection criteria, including skill sets, diversity and experience; recruitment process; orientation
Board Leadership	Selection of board chair; separation of chair and chief executive roles or appointment of "lead" outside director; selection of committee chairs; emergency operation mode
Director Compensation	Composition of compensation (stock, options, cash); basis for determining compensation; expense reimbursement
Board Meeting Procedures	Frequency and length of meetings; director attendance expectations; setting agendas; advanced distribution of board materials; executive sessions of independent directors; attendance by nondirectors
Board Performance	Assessment of board's and committees' effectiveness; assessment of individual director performance; limitations on continuing board membership (retirement, etc.); conflicts of interest
Committees	Specific committees formed; committee membership requirements; selection and rotation of members and chairs; meetings; agendas
Board Relationships	Interaction with chief executive; contact with investors, media, suppliers and customers; access to management and employees

Committees

Most boards use committees to fulfil key aspects of their mandate. Astute directors know that the board can't be effective if its committees aren't, yet the presence of an effective committee doesn't allow the board to abdicate its ultimate responsibility. Effective boards monitor committee activities, guarding against a "silo mentality" by ensuring good sharing of information, cross-committee memberships and bringing major decisions to the full board. They also don't allow issues to fall between the cracks, which sometimes happens when each committee assumes another committee is dealing with a matter.

Committees don't need to be, and shouldn't be, set in stone. Leading boards periodically assess and reconstitute their committee structure as circumstances warrant.

Evaluating the Board

Most boards don't do formal self-evaluations. Recent surveys show less than 20 percent do so. A similar proportion of boards formally evaluates the performance of individual directors.

It might be argued that the best boards don't need a formal evaluation process. They perform well and know when change is needed. Other boards benefit greatly from a self-evaluation process. But even effective boards change over time, and a disciplined process for assessing continued performance can be beneficial to keep the board on the right track.

Boards can perform self-evaluations for any of a number of reasons. Some are for the right reason, which simply is to operate at optimum effectiveness and efficiency, doing the best job for shareholders. A wrong reason is to provide a vehicle to oust specific directors for nefarious purposes.

Why don't most boards evaluate themselves? One reason is rather obvious. Directors by definition are highly accomplished, successful individuals, typically well respected and proven in various forums. CEO/chairs of major enterprises, former senior government officials, leading academicians and other directors might not have been subjected to formal evaluations in years. Their stature, record of accomplishment and ego all argue against evaluation.

Despite an inherent distaste, many boards employing a self-assessment process found it has indeed made individual directors and the board as a whole much better. Board members have an accurate perspective on their peers' performance and contribution, and are well positioned to provide meaningful input. If done well, the process is constructive and motivates positive change.

The experience of one board is telling. Virtually all directors were outstanding individuals, but they rated performance of the board as a whole as poor. While the abilities of directors were excellent, individual performance was no better than average. The assessment process identified dysfunctional board dynamics and shortcomings in ability to function as a team.

Self-evaluation best practice encompasses the following guidance:

- Each director should assess his/her own individual performance, that of each other director and that of the board as a whole.
- Categories on which performance is assessed must be directly relevant to successful boardroom dynamics. See Exhibit 8.2 for a few examples.

- To be effective, the evaluation process needs the support of the chair and/or lead or similar leading independent director.
- The clear and accepted objective must be to improve director and board performance, and not allow the process to pit one director against another. Typically ratings are by category by director, so each director sees how other (unidentified) board members rate his/her performance. This provides each individual with not only a composite rating, but also the range of ratings by category, as well as qualitative input.
- Recognizing sensitivities, feedback should be compiled confidentially, and provided only to the individual director and a lead type director or governance committee.
- Consider using outside consultants to work with the board to determine rating categories, develop evaluation forms, receive and consolidate results, and communicate individual and group feedback.

Objective feedback can be invaluable even to seasoned directors. The saying "perception is reality" applies to how board members see their peers, and a vehicle to share perceptions can be enlightening and extremely helpful to board success.

One CEO/chair reminds his fellow board members, "Being a director is a job, not a privilege, and every job should be evaluated." This director walks the talk, having instituted 360-degree evaluations in his company, including his own CEO role and that of the board, and makes known his personal policy of not joining any board that doesn't use board self-evaluations.

Exhibit 8.2: Factors to Be Evaluated

Board Performance

- Whether key responsibilities noted in the charter were carried out
- Adequacy and timeliness of information received
- Appropriateness of meeting agendas and meeting time allotted
- How well directors worked together, appropriateness of communication and discussion, degree of consensus achieved on key issues, etc.
- Degree of compliance with any membership characteristics (e.g., majority of independent directors)

- Overall level of board's effectiveness

Individual Director Performance

- Meeting attendance rates
- Degree of preparation
- Active participation during meetings
- Ability to communicate and express ideas
- Willingness to listen and acknowledge other viewpoints
- Understanding of company and industry
- Ability to work with directors and management
- What the director does well
- What the director should do differently

- Overall level of contribution

Renewing the Board

Boards need new directors to bring needed new skills, expertise and experiences. In the past, the CEO/chair usually took the lead in identifying and recruiting new directors, sometimes resulting in a board filled with cronies and lacking independence to take needed action. The clear trend now is for boards to appoint nominating or governance committees of independent directors to identify and recommend new board members.

Even with a nominating committee, there's an inherent danger in selecting people already known through directors' business and social experience, which can limit choices. A disciplined and robust process of identifying attributes needed in a new director is crucial, to bring missing skills or knowledge or a perspective needed for today's and tomorrow's issues. And certainly a CEO's nominees might be just right for the board and should be thoughtfully considered. One director puts it this way: "They are among the pack, but not favored."

Orientation of new directors is vital. Many directors polled believe it takes much too long for new board members to contribute—a number of experienced directors mentioning three years. Most say new director orientation programs are not effective. Orientation needs to provide better briefing on the company and its businesses and industries, organization, people, strategies, key issues and risks. Some boards provide orientation manuals, arrange for visits to operating sites or provide formal support, including board mentors.

Commitment

Some board members show up at four meetings a year and otherwise make little time available for board business. Some directors come unprepared, don't actively participate and even doze off at board meetings. Fortunately, these are the exception, and they're seldom tolerated in today's environment.

Directors see a clear link between effective boards and board members who make a significant commitment of time and energy. How much time? Attendance at every board and relevant committee meeting is a start. But it's not nearly enough. Seasoned directors say:

- Directors can't be disengaged between meetings. They need to spend time at the company, with customers and suppliers. They must do this to know the business well enough to add value. Indeed, one successful retailer requires its directors to fulfil a "quota" of store visits monthly.
- Meeting four times a year is simply not enough to deal with the complexities of business today.

One observer tells of a company where each director is expected to spend fully 50 days a year on board business—counting board and committee meetings and work done in between. A director says making that commitment would preclude active chief executives from serving on other boards, which is unthinkable because those individuals are "better able than most to initiate critically needed change." It's been reported that directors of a large U.S. company spend an average of 25 days each year on board business. There's no magic number, but one thing becomes clear—in most cases more time than currently spent is needed.

Also clear is that director compensation needs to be revisited as demands on time and availability increase. Time and again directors and thought leaders argued that directors need to be paid more. Some companies have begun making adjustments, but many others have not.

Can someone serving on many boards be effective? Some favor limits on the number, and some board charters set guidelines. Each board must decide for itself what time commitment is needed. One experienced director notes that if the necessary commitment is met, in terms of time, energy and contribution, the numbers usually take care of themselves.

Should there be term or age limits? Most observers believe age is best dealt with on a case-by-case basis. When questioned about length of service, a number of directors came forth with the timeframe of 10 to 15 years as providing a balance between taking advantage of knowledge and experience on the one hand, and keeping the board fresh on the other.

A Final Word

Directors, more than any other group, have an extraordinary opportunity to enhance shareholder value through their diligent and proactive oversight. Directors can make a difference, but—like any worthwhile endeavor—doing so isn't easy. Unless board members work well together, the company won't gain the requisite benefits. In today's world, the right board membership, with the right dynamics, can make all the difference.

APPENDIX A
SELF-ASSESSMENT GUIDE

The following Guide summarizes key principles and practices discussed in this report, and is provided for your use in assessing your board's performance. You may find it useful to rate the extent to which your board complies with each statement, on a scale where 1 = Strongly Disagree and 5 = Strongly Agree. If the practice is not being followed or if the rating is below what you consider acceptable, space is provided to note steps your board should take to raise performance. You also might want to use that column to capture any personal actions you wish to take.

PRINCIPAL COMPONENTS OF EFFECTIVE GOVERNANCE	Board Rating (1-5)	FOLLOW-UP ACTIONS (Including any personal plans)
Strategy and Planning **Your board:** Brings **insight, knowledge, judgment and analytical skill** to the strategic planning process, and **directors' expertise, perspectives and judgment are valued and embraced** by management		
Ensures **strategic planning discussions occur in appropriate venues**, with the **atmosphere, format and alloted time** to do the job right		

PRINCIPAL COMPONENTS OF EFFECTIVE GOVERNANCE	Board Rating (1-5)	FOLLOW-UP ACTIONS (Including any personal plans)
Aggressively and constructively debates proposed strategy, considering critical issues such as emerging customer preferences, technology risks and opportunities, quality issues, supply chain, e-commerce and new product and market opportunities		
Obtains internal and external **information needed** to evaluate the strategy, including information on risk factors, interdependencies, resources, strategic alliances/ partnerships, technology issues and competitive intelligence		
Ensures the **strategy planning process** is **sufficiently robust** and considers a **range of strategic alternatives**		
Recognizes the **extent of planned change**—incremental, substantial or transformational—and **is comfortable with it**		
Evaluates past strategy success or failure, and uses the lessons learned		

PRINCIPAL COMPONENTS OF EFFECTIVE GOVERNANCE	Board Rating (1-5)	FOLLOW-UP ACTIONS (Including any personal plans)
Assesses best, worst and most-likely case **scenarios of** the **proposed strategy**		
Is **comfortable with plans and processes for strategy implementation** —including need for organizational realignment, use of e-business, human resources and incentive/reward systems, and risk management and information systems—and **provides operational and tactical guidance to management**		
Reaches agreement with management on performance measurements, aligned to value drivers and the strategy, **to be used in assessing success** of the strategy's implementation		
Risk Management **Your board:** Is **satisfied management has** in place an **effective risk architecture** to identify risk, measure its potential impact and do what's necessary to proactively manage it		

PRINCIPAL COMPONENTS OF EFFECTIVE GOVERNANCE	Board Rating (1-5)	FOLLOW-UP ACTIONS (Including any personal plans)
Ensures the risk management **process** effectively **aligns** the **strategy, business objectives, risks, actions and controls**		
Ensures the **process** not only has **identified current risks**, but also **identifies new risks as they emerge**		
Is sure **everyone shares the conceptual definition** of risk, with **common terminology** used in everyday communication		
Is comfortable the risk **architecture covers all risk categories**—operations, financial reporting and compliance		
Is comfortable that **roles and responsibilities for risk management** are **clearly defined**, with **line managers directly responsible,** and **risk or compliance officer** and **internal audit in support/monitoring roles**		

PRINCIPAL COMPONENTS OF EFFECTIVE GOVERNANCE	Board Rating (1-5)	FOLLOW-UP ACTIONS (Including any personal plans)
Has made sure **line management embraces responsibility** for risk management, with **cascading responsibility** from the top throughout the organization, and with effective **communication and accountability**		
Sees that **management maintains a culture** that **rewards** the **recognition, communication** and **management of risks,** with human resource **performance assessment, compensation and incentive programs linked** to **managers' risk management performance**		
Is **apprised timely** of all **significant risks**, and is **comfortable with what management is doing to manage** them		
Tone at the Top **Your board:** Is satisfied **senior management** has **established** through word and action the **desired value-based culture**, and culture permeates the organization		
Ensures the **company** selectively **recruits people** with **track records** of **performance** and **values** consistent with the company's desired culture, and **reinforces** appropriate **behavior through** effective **human resources practices**, including remuneration		

PRINCIPAL COMPONENTS OF EFFECTIVE GOVERNANCE	Board Rating (1-5)	FOLLOW-UP ACTIONS (Including any personal plans)
Ensures **management has put in place an appropriate code of conduct, adheres to it** and **sees** that **all personnel understand its terms, relevance** and **importance**		
Makes sure **appropriate personnel are required to confirm** in writing that they **comply** with the code, and ethics **violations are taken seriously** and **reflected in training** and **communications**		
Is satisfied **effective supplementary communication channels** (such as hotlines, ombudspersons, legal or compliance officers) **exist** through which **personnel can get help with ethics issues**		
Recognizes that management's actions drive behavior, and **holds line management accountable for living corporate values** and **maintaining ethical standards**		
Members have ongoing direct contact with customers, suppliers and **people throughout the company,** determining for themselves what attitudes and values are espoused by managers and how the values are embraced by the rank and file		

PRINCIPAL COMPONENTS OF EFFECTIVE GOVERNANCE	**Board Rating (1-5)**	**FOLLOW-UP ACTIONS (Including any personal plans)**
Recognizes the role a counterparty's values play in mergers, acquisitions and alliances, **specifically considers ethical values** as it debates the merits **of proposed transactions,** and then ensures **management effectively integrates** the **cultures**		
Members clearly **demonstrate the required ethical values**, both at the board table and in every contact with the company and its stakeholders		
Measuring and Monitoring Performance **Your board:** Ensures performance **measures** used by management and reported to the **board are linked to tactics** and **strategy** and to the real **value drivers**		
Ensures **performance measures balance financial** and **nonfinancial** metrics, **include forward-looking** measures and enable **benchmarking against competitors, peers** and **best practice companies**		

PRINCIPAL COMPONENTS OF EFFECTIVE GOVERNANCE	**Board Rating (1-5)**	**FOLLOW-UP ACTIONS (Including any personal plans)**
Is satisfied **measures appropriately balance** operations, customer, employee, and finance/shareholder **key scorecard categories,** and **cover key value chain processes**		
Is satisfied **performance goals and targets effectively motivate**—they're set to aggressively drive growth, without being so unreachable as to be a disincentive		
Is comfortable **information systems provide** both **management** and the **board timely** critical **metrics,** of relevant scope and depth to proactively **manage/monitor the business**		
Supplements management-supplied data with hands on drill-down capabilities, is **comfortable with the information reliability** and regularly **validates information/analyses** through **direct contact with customers, suppliers, employees** and others		
Is satisfied **measures directly link to rewards** at all organization levels, tying to both unit and company-wide goals		

PRINCIPAL COMPONENTS OF EFFECTIVE GOVERNANCE	Board Rating (1-5)	FOLLOW-UP ACTIONS (Including any personal plans)
Early and continuously **examines with management shortfalls/progress toward meeting targets**, and works cohesively and proactively with management in making course corrections		
Transformational Transactions **Your board:** Becomes entirely **comfortable with business reasons for** any proposed **merger or acquisition** and with the **potential deal's links with** the **company's strategy**		
Makes sure **management has** the **real market** and **competitor research** and **facts, critically assesses underlying** strategic and market **assumptions**, and looks critically at internal and external **management** and **support expertise**		
Ensures the potential **acquisition plays to the enterprise's competencies or brings truly new ones**, that the proposal **analyzes critical risks and opportunities** presented by different economic and competitive scenarios, and that it **maps target strategies and tactics to** these **scenarios**		

PRINCIPAL COMPONENTS OF EFFECTIVE GOVERNANCE	Board Rating (1-5)	FOLLOW-UP ACTIONS (Including any personal plans)
Ensures the **due diligence process** is well **coordinated** between **experienced acquisition teams** and subject matter experts in market analysis, operations, technology, finance, human resources, treasury and legal, and these teams use sufficiently detailed **operational and financial information, continually updated through closing**		
Is comfortable with **management's ability to develop** and **execute** the **integration plan**, with particular **focus on early integration actions that drive value**, and that they can **effect** the **changes needed** to make the deal pay off		
Sees that **implementation plans** clearly **define key management roles** and **relationships**, encompass organization **structure decisions based on skill sets and operating style**, are grounded in a **full understanding of** the **different cultures** and **create** a **desired behavior pattern that will support** the **combined businesses' strategies and values**		
Conducts **post-transaction evaluations** — particularly those failing to improve shareholder value as promised— **assessing management's plans to ensure future success**		

PRINCIPAL COMPONENTS OF EFFECTIVE GOVERNANCE	Board Rating (1-5)	FOLLOW-UP ACTIONS (Including any personal plans)
When divesting, **recognizes disparate incentives** of managers and investment bankers versus shareholders, **understands to whom the business is most valuable** and **takes timely personnel actions to** preserve and **maximize sale value**		
Makes sure **joint ventures/alliances** being considered **involve the right partners**, are **structured properly** and are subject to **intensive due diligence**		
Thoroughly **reviews major capital expenditures** for **strategic link, relative priority** and alignment with **financial return requisites**, and then **evaluates ultimate outcomes** as input to future decisions		
Has the courage to walk away from a bad deal**, regardless of sunk cost or external pressures**		

PRINCIPAL COMPONENTS OF EFFECTIVE GOVERNANCE	Board Rating (1-5)	FOLLOW-UP ACTIONS (Including any personal plans)
Management Evaluation, Compensation and Succession Planning **Your board:** Establishes **clear-cut, comprehensive performance criteria, metrics and qualitative measures** in evaluating the CEO's performance, **linked to corporate strategy** and **encompassing** both **short- and long-term company and personal goals**		
Continually monitors performance, providing **clear, constructive feedback** at **interim points** as well as a formal annual review		
Has **established a collegial** working **partnership** with the CEO, yet **balances and differentiates** between **discussion**, **guidance** and **directive** comments		
Evaluates the **CEO's progress in meeting both quantitative objectives and qualitative ones** such as **developing** competent, motivated, balanced and team-oriented **leadership throughout** the **organization,** and **setting** the **right ethical values and tone at the top**		

PRINCIPAL COMPONENTS OF EFFECTIVE GOVERNANCE	Board Rating (1-5)	FOLLOW-UP ACTIONS (Including any personal plans)
Designs **rewards** that will **drive achievement** of both short- and long-term **corporate goals, incenting** the **CEO** and **senior management to make hard choices** for the company's long-term prosperity, and **linking incentives** not only to financial performance but also to **forward-looking indicators of business health** such as new customers, distribution channels and product introductions		
Takes steps to **retain** and **attract** the **best talent, effectively balancing** compensation-related **pressure between** forceful, in-demand **executives** and **analysts and investors**		
Sees that **evaluation/compensation decisions** are **formulated by** truly independent **directors**, who are **in no way beholden to management**		
Has in place the **right evaluative mechanisms**, and has the **courage and conviction to make tough decisions**, including the **willingness to replace a chief executive** whose performance is not acceptable		

PRINCIPAL COMPONENTS OF EFFECTIVE GOVERNANCE	Board Rating (1-5)	FOLLOW-UP ACTIONS (Including any personal plans)
Gives sufficient attention to **evaluation of senior executives** below the CEO, ensuring **development and retention of essential talent—**top performers and underachievers are identified, rewards or remedial steps/removal initiated as needed and **directors meet senior managers** to know firsthand individuals who may one day lead the company		
Is comfortable with **succession plans**, and with the **process for identifying a new chief executive to lead the company** should that become necessary		
Telling the World **Your board:** Recognizes the threat of **earnings manipulation** and **other forces/ sources affecting annual or interim financial reporting,** has the **expertise and wherewithal to ask insightful questions**, and **considers** results in light of **benchmarks, performance measures** and **economic data**		
Recognizes the relevance of **operating information that management releases, monitors its reporting** and **challenges information accuracy** by **probing controls** over and **verifications** of the to-be-reported information		

PRINCIPAL COMPONENTS OF EFFECTIVE GOVERNANCE	**Board Rating (1-5)**	**FOLLOW-UP ACTIONS (Including any personal plans)**
Is comfortable **communications policies and processes encompass best practice** such as a **clearly designated** and skilled **spokesperson**, explicit **prohibitions on speaking on behalf of the company** or **sharing information externally**, and mechanisms to **monitor** and **enforce compliance**		
Makes sure **stakeholders are treated equally,** with **information disseminated to interested parties**—analysts, investors, the media—**at the same time**, properly **harnessing technology** and **protecting against its abuse**		
Scrutinizes **processes surrounding confidentiality of unannounced deals** or developments, **ensuring both regulatory compliance** and respect for the **rights of all interested parties** and ensuring the company's **ability to track who knows what and when**		
Ensures **communications policies cover board members themselves** so that all company communications move through designated channels		

PRINCIPAL COMPONENTS OF EFFECTIVE GOVERNANCE	Board Rating (1-5)	FOLLOW-UP ACTIONS (Including any personal plans)
Board Dynamics **Your board:** Membership has a **sufficiently independent** voice, **in no way beholden to the chief executive**, and **consistently ready to constructively challenge** the **management team**		
Members possess the **requisite characteristics**, such as integrity, judgment, credibility, trustworthiness, strategic thinking, intuition, vision, industry knowledge, communication (including listening) skills, decision-making ability, interpersonal skills, willingness to actively participate and ability to constructively handle conflict		
Is the **right size**, bringing the **requisite knowledge, abilities and skills** to the table in a **group small enough to act cohesively**		
Operates in an **atmosphere of openness** and **trust,** where directors feel **free to speak their minds** and **pursue issues to conclusion**		
Members bring **fresh ideas, creativity, constructive tension** and **feedback, balancing thought** and **thoroughness with speed** and **decisiveness**		

PRINCIPAL COMPONENTS OF EFFECTIVE GOVERNANCE	**Board Rating (1-5)**	**FOLLOW-UP ACTIONS (Including any personal plans)**
The **CEO truly believes** that **he/she can learn from the board**		
Meetings are effective, with **advance buy-in on the agenda**, the **right amount of good advance material distributed timely**, the **tough issues put first, little bureaucracy, limited presentations** to allow full dialogue, **cushion for additional time** to conclude on major issues, and with more attention given to the future than the past		
Members, recognizing that relationships are not developed solely in the boardroom, **devote time to frequent off-line interactions** necessary to **establish trust among members** and with **management**		
Members who are **nonmanagement directors regularly meet separately,** with issues/guidance/concerns communicated to the chief executive, and **support one another** as appropriate, especially during contentious board meetings		

PRINCIPAL COMPONENTS OF EFFECTIVE GOVERNANCE	Board Rating (1-5)	FOLLOW-UP ACTIONS (Including any personal plans)
Regularly evaluates performance of both the **board as a whole** and **individual directors**, and takes decisive corrective action		
Has designated **independent directors to nominate new members**, first **identifying needed skills/attributes** and then **seeking the best candidates** who will have the **capacity, desire** and **commitment** to carry out their responsibilities		

APPENDIX B
PROJECT METHOD

This report is based on a review of corporate governance literature, a survey, interviews and the knowledge and experience of PricewaterhouseCoopers' professionals.

Literature Search

The project team reviewed literature on corporate governance in major developed countries. This included recommendations and guidelines issued by national and international organizations (e.g., stock exchanges, legal associations, the Organization for Economic Cooperation and Development), surveys on board practices published by organizations such as the National Association of Corporate Directors and the American Society of Corporate Secretaries, and business publications addressing board responsibilities. Some of the most informative sources drawn on for this report are listed in Appendix C.

Survey

We surveyed board directors of 126 public companies, judgmentally selected across diverse industries from nine countries: Australia, Canada, France, Hong Kong, The Netherlands, New Zealand, Singapore, the United Kingdom and the United States. For the companies selected, the board chair and audit committee chair—if an audit committee existed—were identified. For approximately half the companies, another nonexecutive director also was identified. In total, 297 questionnaires were distributed.

The survey focused particularly on board involvement relative to:

- The importance the board places on major corporate governance responsibilities
- The extent of board involvement in each area (e.g., *do* versus *review* versus *approve*)
- The degree of satisfaction with the information the board receives to allow it to monitor each area

Audit committee chairs (or board chairs, where no audit committee existed) were asked additional questions about their roles, responsibilities and activities in monitoring financial reporting and interacting with independent and internal auditors.

Seventy-two directors (or 24 percent) returned completed surveys: 26 board chairs, 35 audit committee chairs and 11 nonexecutive directors who were neither board nor audit committee chairs. We gratefully acknowledge these directors and thank them for the time, effort and care with which they provided their information.

Interview Activities

We conducted interviews with directors and corporate governance thought leaders. An interview guide was used as a starting point, with the interviewee providing whatever information he or she deemed pertinent. We acknowledge and greatly appreciate all of these individuals who gave their time and shared their experiences, expertise, views and perspectives.

Directors and Thought Leaders	*Affiliations*
Dr. Carolyn Kay Brancato	Director, The Conference Board's Global Corporate Governance Research Center
John Christian Dahlsen	Solicitor, Corrs, Chambers, Westgarth, and director of Woolworths Limited, Southern Cross Broadcasting (Aust.) Limited, Australia and New Zealand Banking Group Limited, Melbourne Business School Limited
Marina Darling	Director of Argo Investments Limited, Southern Cross Broadcasting (Australia) Limited, National Australia Trustees Limited (subsidiary of the National Australia Bank Limited), Member Federal Taskforce on Industry Self-Regulation, Member Prime Minister's Community Business Partnership
Paul Desarmeaux	CEO, Gascogne Group
William H. Donaldson	Chairman and CEO, Aetna Inc., Co-founder, former Chairman and CEO, Donaldson, Lufkin & Jenrette, former Chairman and CEO, New York Stock Exchange, former U.S. Undersecretary of State and Counsel to the Vice President of the United States, founding Dean and Professor of Management, the Yale School of Management and director of Mail.com, Inc., Bright Horizons Family Solutions Inc. and NEC Corporation (International Advisory Board)

Directors and Thought Leaders	*Affiliations*
Dr. Charles M. Elson	Professor, Stetson University College of Law, Of Counsel, Holland & Knight, and director of Sunbeam Corporation, Nuevo Energy Company, Circon Corporation
Jane Finley	Associate Dean Massey Graduate Business School, Belmont University, and director of Healthcor Holdings Inc.
Louis Foissac	Chairman and CEO, Chemunex
Alain Gilbert	Director of Chemunex
Kayla J. Gillan	General Counsel, California Public Employees' Retirement System (CalPERS)
Hon. Barbara Hackman Franklin	President and CEO, Barbara Franklin Enterprises, former U.S. Secretary of Commerce, and director of The Dow Chemical Company, Aetna, Inc., Guest Services, Inc., Milacron Inc., MedImmune, Inc.
David M. Lawrence, M.D.	Chairman and CEO, Kaiser Foundation Health Plan Inc., and director of Agilent Technologies, Inc., Pacific Gas and Electric Company
Leon Michael L'Huillier	Former CEO of Lion Nathan Australia and director of Woolworths Limited, MLC Limited, Fortis Australia Limited
Helen A. Lynch	Director of Coles Myer Limited, Southcorp Limited, Westpac Banking Corporation, OPSM Protector Limited, Superannuation Funds Management Corporation of South Australia
John W. Melbourn, CBE	Deputy Chairman 3i Group plc and director of Tesco plc
Sir Brian Moffat	Chairman of Corus Group plc and director of HSBC Holdings plc, Enterprise Oil plc
Shaun F. O'Malley	Former Chairman, Price Waterhouse LLP and director of Vlasic Foods International Inc., Horace Mann Educators Corporation, Finance Company of Pennsylvania

Directors and Thought Leaders	***Affiliations***
Conrad J. Oort	Former Treasurer General of the Dutch Ministry of Finance, Non-executive Chairman of KLM Royal Dutch Airlines and of Robeco Group N.V. and director of ABN AMRO Bank, Royal Philips Electronics N.V., Royal KPN N.V., TNT Post Group N.V.
Roger W. Raber	President and CEO, National Association of Corporate Directors
William K. Reilly	President and CEO, Aqua International Partners, LLP, director of DuPont E.I. De Nemours & Co., Conoco Inc., Evergreen Holdings, Inc., Royal Caribbean International, Inc.
Kenneth Roman	Director of Compaq Computer Corporation, Brunswick Corporation, Coty, Inc., Nelson Communications Inc., PennCorp Financial Group, Inc.
A.A. Sommer, Jr.	Chairman, Public Oversight Board, American Institute of Certified Public Accountants, Counsel and former partner of Morgan Lewis & Bockius, LLP and former Commissioner, Securities and Exchange Commission
Dr. Paula Stern	President, The Stern Group, Inc., member of the President's Advisory Committee for Trade Policy and Negotiation, Former Chairwoman, U.S. International Trade Commission and director of Wal-Mart Stores, Inc., Avon Products, Inc., CBS, Inc., Harcourt General, Inc., Infinity Broadcasting Corporation
Lynn E. Turner	Chief Accountant, Securities and Exchange Commission
James R. Ukropina	Partner, O'Melveny & Myers, Vice Chair of the Board of Trustees of Stanford University, and director of Lockheed Martin Corporation, Pacific Life Insurance Company
Peter Wade	Chairman of CSL Limited and director of Tabcorp Holdings Limited
Catherine Walter	Former Managing Partner, Clayton Utz, Solicitors and director of Orica Ltd., National Australia Bank Ltd., Australian Stock Exchange, Vodafone Pacific Pty Ltd.

PricewaterhouseCoopers Contributors

This report also represents the efforts, knowledge and experience of many PricewaterhouseCoopers people from around the world:

Elizabeth A. Alexander
Harvey J. Bazaar
Myra D. Cleary
Philip J. Clements
John W. Copley
Eric Dugelay
Frances C. Engoron
Daniel Fesson
Laurent Gravier
Govind Gupta
Ian Hollows
Peter M. Horoszko
Betty Hutchison
Ruud Kok
Kathleen H. Leibfried
Susan Lowry
Richard J. Machold
Roger McArt
David L. McLean
Grady E. Means
Adil Nariman
Judith Nicholl
Bernadette Nye
Michael T. O'Brien
Allen Pfeiffer
Paul E. Platten
Lawrence A. Ponemon
Frank J. Raiti
Rajendra M. Riswadkar
Robert Rudloff
Donniel S. Schulman
James F. Spitler
Steven J. Stampf
Derek Trendell

We also gratefully acknowledge the contributions of former PricewaterhouseCoopers colleagues, Robert L. Gorvett, who as the initial project partner developed the research plan, and Jeffrey K. Rader, who served as a member of the core project team.

APPENDIX C
SELECTED BIBLIOGRAPHY

The following is a selection of key sources, including books, reports, articles and PricewaterhouseCoopers publications and white papers from which we drew:

American Bar Association, *Corporate Director's Guidebook, Second Edition*, 1994.

The American Law Institute, *Principles of Corporate Governance: Analysis and Recommendations*, 1994.

American Society of Corporate Secretaries, Inc., *Current Board Practices, Second Study*, March 1998.

Bank of Montreal, *1997, 1998 and 1999 Annual Reports and Proxy Circulars.*

Berenbeim, Ronald E., *Global Corporate Ethics Practices: A Developing Consensus*, The Conference Board, 1999.

The Business Round Table, *Statement on Corporate Governance*, September 1997.

California Public Employees' Retirement System, *U.S. Corporate Governance Core Principles and Guidelines*, April 1998.

Canadian Institute of Chartered Accountants, *Corporate Governance - A Review of Disclosure Practices in Canada*, December 1997.

Canadian Institute of Chartered Accountants, *Guidance for Directors - Dealing with Risk in the Boardroom - Draft for Comment*, August 1999.

Canadian Institute of Chartered Accountants, *Guidance for Directors - Governance Processes for Control*, December 1995.

CCAF-FCVI Inc., *Information - the Currency of Corporate Governance*, 1997.

Committee on Corporate Governance - Final Report, January 1998.

Committee of Sponsoring Organizations of the Treadway Commission, *Internal Control – Integrated Framework*, 1992.

Corporate Governance - A Guide for Investment Managers and Corporations, Second Edition, Australian Investment Managers' Association, July 1997.

Corporate Governance - Improving Competitiveness and Access to Capital in Global Markets, A Report to the OECD by the Business Sector Advisory Group on Corporate Governance, April 1998.

Donaldson, Gordon, "A New Tool for Boards: The Strategic Audit," *Harvard Business Review*, July-August 1995, pp. 99-107.

The Economist Intelligence Unit Limited and PricewaterhouseCoopers, *Corporate Performance Management - Ensuring Strategy Implementation*, 1999.

Gregory, Holly J. and Forminard, Elizabeth R., *International Comparison of Board "Best Practices,"* Weil, Gotshal & Manges, LLP, March 1998.

Hermanson, Dana R. and Hermanson, Heather M., "The 'Balanced Scorecard' as a Board Tool," *The Corporate Board*, January/February 1997, pp. 17-21.

International Capital Markets Group, *Who Holds the Reins? An Overview of Corporate Governance Practice in Japan, Germany, France, United States of America, Canada and the United Kingdom*, June 1995.

The King Report on Corporate Governance, The Institute of Directors in Southern Africa, November 1994.

Leighton, David S.R. and Thain, Donald H., "Why Boards Fail," *The Corporate Board*, September/October 1997, pp. 6-11.

Lorsch, Jay W. and Lipton, Martin, "The Lead Director," *Directors & Boards*, Spring 1993, pp. 28-29.

National Association of Corporate Directors, *1999 Annual Corporate Governance Conference*, October 17-19, 1999.

National Association of Corporate Directors, *1999-2000 Public Company Governance Survey*, October 1999.

National Association of Corporate Directors, *The NACD Board Guidelines*, 1999.

Pound, John, "The Promise of the Governed Corporation," *Harvard Business Review*, March-April 1995, pp. 89-98.

PricewaterhouseCoopers, *Corporate Strategy for the New Millennium*, 1999.

PricewaterhouseCoopers, *Managing Corporate Performance Today and Tomorrow*, 1999.

Price Waterhouse, *Converging Cultures - Trends in European Corporate Governance*, April 1997.

Report of the Committee on the Financial Aspects of Corporate Governance: The Code of Best Practice, December 1992.

Report on Corporate Governance, 1999 - Five years to the Dey, Toronto Stock Exchange and Institute of Corporate Directors, June 1999.

Steinberg, Richard M., "No, It Couldn't Happen Here," *Management Review*, September 1998, p. 70.

Sullivan, Katherine McG. and Gregory, Holly J., "Board Self-Assessment," *The Corporate Board*, November/December 1995, pp. 6-11.

"Where Were the Directors?" Guidelines for Improved Corporate Governance in Canada, *Report of the Toronto Stock Exchange Committee on Corporate Governance in Canada*, December 1994.

IIA Research Foundation Board of Trustees 1999/2000

IIA Research Foundation Board of Research Advisors 1999/2000

Chairman

Stephen A. Doherty, CPA, CISA, *Credit Lyonnais Americas*

Members

Charles H. "Bud" Allen, CBA, CISA, *Wilmington Trust Company*
Betty Ann Blandon, CIA, CPA, *Tandy Corporation*
LeRoy E. Bookal, CIA, CMA, *Texaco, Inc.*
Carolyn Y. Buford, CBA, CFE, CFSA, *Fannie Mae*
Gareth Evans, MIIA, *England Intervention Board for Agricultural Produce*
John F. Garry, CIA, CPA, CISA, *PricewaterhouseCoopers LLP*
David Hodgson, CPA, *PricewaterhouseCoopers LLP*
Kasey K. Kiplinger, CIA, CGFM, *Iowa Workforce Development Administration Center*
Joy S. LaBar, CIA, CPA, *Oklahoma City*
Gary J. Mann, PhD, CPA, *University of Texas at El Paso*
Betty L. McPhilimy, CIA, CPA, CFE, *Northwestern University*
Donna T. Moy, CPA
Jane F. Mutchler, PhD, CPA, *Georgia State University School of Accountancy*
Claire Beth Nilsen, CRCM, CFE, CFSA, *Philadelphia Stock Exchange*
Heriot Calder Prentice, *Deloitte & Touche LLP*
Mark R. Radde, CIA, CPA, *Arthur Andersen LLP*
Tage Rasmussen, *Aarhus School of Business*
Mark L. Salamasick, CISA, CDP, CSP, *Bank of America*
Adelheid M. Schilliger, *ABB Asea Brown Boveri LTD*
Jay H. Stott, CIA, *Fidelity Investments*
Frank Robert Tallerico, CIA, CPA, *Pioneer Hi Bred International, Inc.*
James H. Thompson, CIA, *James Thompson & Associates*
Curtis C. Verschoor, CIA, CMA, CPA, CFP, *DePaul University*
Scott D. White, CIA, CBA, CISA, CTA, *Sun Life of Canada*

IIA Staff Liaison

Susan B. Lione, CIA, *Senior Manager of Research*

For more than 25 years, The Institute of Internal Auditors has looked to The Research Foundation to define leading internal audit practices and to promote the profession to academic institutions. The Foundation's board of trustees recently redefined their mission as:

"To be the recognized leader in sponsoring and disseminating research, to assist and guide internal auditing professionals and others, in the areas of risk management, controls, governance processes and audit practices."

The Research Foundation is committed to:
- Defining internal auditing practices as performed by global leaders in research reports.
- Educating practitioners, educators, and the general public about the merits of internal auditing.
- Distributing materials on the benefits of internal auditing to organizational leaders and clients.

To continue to benefit from this ongoing effort and to help The Foundation fund top-quality research studies and educational programs for internal auditors worldwide, join the Master Key Program. For $1,000, your organization can become a subscriber and receive all Research Foundation publications and research reports as soon as they come off the press.

2001 Master Key subscribers will receive titles like:
- *An e-Risk Primer*
- *Independence and Objectivity: A Framework for Internal Auditors*
- *Internal Auditing Reengineering: Survey, Model, and Best Practices*
- *Enterprise Risk Management: Trends and Emerging Practices*
- *Effective Compliance Systems*
- *Fraud and Its Deterrence*
- *Value Added Services of Internal Auditors*

To subscribe to the Master Key Program, call: +1-407-830-7600, Ext. 279 or e-mail: research@theiia.org

---

Count on The IIA Research Foundation to help you perfect your profession and empower your success. Subscribe today.

To order individual copies of Research Foundation reports:
Online: www.theiia.org under The IIA
E-mail: iiapubs@pbd.org